RMS Queen Eli
~ From Victory to Valhalla

Foreword

About twenty years ago, when it was announced that the *Queen Elizabeth* was to follow her older sister into retirement, Noel Mostert wrote an article for the "US Travel News" called "Farewell to the Great Ships" in which he said, "The two older *Queens* undoubtedly will *always remain* the finest ships ever built," and these words have reverberated through my mind over the years whenever I have thought about my last command. After mentioning the 500,000 ton tankers being built at that time he concluded: "No tanker no matter its size, could ever carry the visual impact of these two magnificent ships, especially when seen at speed, flinging the North Atlantic aside in huge combers. Their whole line, one of power and splendour, oceanic palaces of staggering dimensions."

Many people tend to compare the *Queen Elizabeth* unfavourably with the *Queen Mary* when it comes to the internal decoration of her public rooms but it must be remembered that whilst her decorations were designed in the late 1930s they had to be completed in that period of austerity and material shortages that followed World War Two.

But to me, the *Queen Elizabeth* was always a ship of great dignity, and the beauty and symmetry of her lines when viewed from the beam have never been surpassed.

Her destruction by fire in Hong Kong harbour on 9th January 1972 was a great tragedy but as I said at the time, at least she had a Viking's funeral, and if there is a Valhalla for ships she will occupy a place of honour, as we who knew her, in fair weather and foul, salute her.

So it is with great pleasure that I introduce David Hutchings' book, which I hope will revive many memories of the ship which played such an important part in my life.

Geoffrey T. Marr. DSC, RD, CDR, RNR (Retd.)
Commodore (retired) of the Cunard Line and last captain of RMS *QUEEN ELIZABETH*.

Preface

I started work on the rough draught of this book shortly after finishing 'QE2 - a Ship for all Seasons' thinking that I had, by then, simultaneously researched most of the information that I needed for the new volume.

But the more I wrote the more I discovered until this volume grew to become the largest (and a year late in publication because of it) of the ship biographies that I have produced for Kingfisher Publications.

Perhaps this is appropriate. Not only was the *Queen Elizabeth* the largest passenger liner ever built but she also held, for many years, the distinction of being the largest ship in the world. She was also the flagship of 'The Cunard', flying the flag of the Commodore of the world's premier passenger fleet. Surely such an eminent vessel deserves the largest tribute!

The delay in publication has also fortunately meant that the book will also appear in time for Cunard's 150th anniversary, although missing by a few months the 21st anniversary of the ship's final voyage in Cunard service.

And to those readers who have awaited publication (and my wife who suffered the extended authorship!) with patience - thank you.

David F. Hutchings, Lee-on-the-Solent, Hampshire.
June 1990

Front cover: Queen Elizabeth's last departure from New York, 30th October 1968. *Carl House/QE Historical Society*
Inside front cover: The last refuelling at night in Southampton of the *Queen Elizabeth*, 7th November 1968. *R. Bruce-Grice*
Back cover: The most striking feature of the *Queen Elizabeth* was her two red funnels. *Norman Jackman*

© David F. Hutchings & Kingfisher Publications, 1990
ISBN 0 946184 55 0
Typeset by PageMerger, Southampton
Printed by Amadeus Press, Huddersfield, Yorkshire
Cover design by David F. Hutchings

Contents

*To Dorothie (the late Mrs. Geoffrey Marr)
and all other wives of the sea who have patiently waited.*

Published by
Kingfisher Publications
65A The Avenue, Southampton SO1 2TA

Chapter One
The Noble Mission

Her Majesty, Queen Elizabeth, stood on the launch platform that had been decorated in blue and gold. With the Royal Coat of Arms placed centrally its canopy and glass front protected her from the dull September day, the earlier drizzle having fortunately stopped.

Standing discreetly behind the Queen were various dignitaries and officials including Lord Aberconway, chairman of the shipyard which had built the ship that stood before them and Sir Percy Bates, chairman of the shipping company for whom it was being launched. To her right stood two little princesses – her daughters Elizabeth and Margaret Rose, both dressed in rose pink – excitedly looking up at the pencil-slim bow of the huge ship that their mother had come to launch towering 80 feet above them.

Four years and a day had passed since the Queen's predecessor, Queen Mary, had similarly come to Clyde-bank to launch her own very successful namesake that was even now ploughing its way across the North Atlantic at record-breaking speeds.

Now, on Tuesday 27th September 1938, it was the turn of her daughter-in-law, consort of her son King George VI, to stand at the head of the same slipway on which the *Queen Mary* had been built and sent into the Clyde with such genuine national rejoicing. The completion of the *Queen Mary* had symbolised, by the resumption of her interrupted building, the end of the Great Depression in Britain during which millions of people had been forced out of work.

Earlier, thousands of cheering, flag waving children had greeted the Royal party shortly after its arrival and reception at the south end of the jetty a few minutes before 3 pm.

Almost ready for launching, the *Queen Elizabeth*'s raked bow looms above the platform from which Her Majesty Queen Elizabeth will perform the launching ceremony.
Stewart Bale Ltd/Queen Elizabeth Historical Society

As yet without the letters of her name attached 'No. 552' awaits her launch, looming above an as yet quiet shipyard.

Stewart Bale Ltd/Queen Elizabeth Historical Society

However, the excitement that hung over Clydebank that day as the Queen – herself a daughter of Scotland which doubly endeared her to the waiting crowds – approached the launch platform contrasted sharply with the tension that hung over the rest of Europe. It was this tension that had kept the King at home in London at the request of the Prime Minister.

The mood of grim expectancy that gripped Great Britain and its continental neighbours had found its roots a few months earlier when the dictatorial German Chancellor, Adolf Hitler, had ordered his troops to march into Austria as part of his politically coerced annexation of that country, thus making it a satellite of his expanding Nazi empire.

Now, in September of 1938, in a crescendo of fear, tyranny and propaganda he had cast his hungry eyes eastwards towards the young state of Czechoslovakia claiming its western province of Sudetanland as Germany's, using as his pretext the falsely laid charge that the German minority living there were being persecuted by the Czech government.

Hitler's secret aim, however, was the eventual destruction and take-over of Czechoslovakia as an independent state, and the political crisis that was developing – even as the Queen stepped forward to launch the largest liner in the world – would lead Western Europe to turn its back on Czechoslovakia in a futile attempt to appease Hitler in the hope of avoiding a European war. (This would be all neatly expressed a few days later in the Munich Agreement which assured 'peace in our time'.)

Even so, war seemed to be very much a likelihood. A mobilisation that had been ordered had even gone so far as the secret withdrawal from service of many liners in readiness for a possible outbreak of hostilities. The Cunard's *Aquitania* was so affected, eventually arriving in Port Said laden with troops after a mysterious and sudden disappearance from her North Atlantic duties.

The King had, however, sent a message which the Queen, after the playing of the National Anthem and being presented with a bouquet, incorporated into her speech that she delivered after hearing a speech of welcome:

Queen Elizabeth, Princess Elizabeth and the then Mr Stephen Pigott, watch the launch of the *Queen Elizabeth* at the Clydebank on 27th September 1938.

Shipbuilding and Shipping Record

'I thank you for the kind words of your address,' she said, and continued: 'the King has asked me to assure you of the deep regret he feels at finding himself compelled, at the last moment, to cancel his journey to Clydebank for the launching of the new liner. This ceremony, to which many thousands have looked forward so eagerly, must now take place under circumstances far different from those for which they had hoped.

'I have, however, a message for you from the King. He bids the people of this country to be of good cheer in spite of the dark clouds hanging over them and indeed over the whole world. He knows, too, that they will place entire confidence in their leaders, who, under God's providence, are striving their utmost to find a just and peaceful solution of the grave problems which confront them.' The rest of the speech was the words that the King would have spoken had he been present.

'The very sight of this great ship brings home to us how necessary it is for the welfare of man that the arts of peaceful industry should continue – arts in the promotion of which Scotland has long held a leading place. The city of Glasgow has been for Scotland the principal doorway opening upon the world. The narrow waters of the Clyde have been the cradle of a large part of Britain's mercantile marine, so it is right that from here should go our foremost achievement in that she is the greatest ship that plies to and fro across the Atlantic, like a shuttle in a mighty loom weaving a fabric of friendship and understanding between the people of Britain and the peoples of the United States.

It is fitting that the noblest vessel ever built in Britain, and built with the help of her Government and people, should be dedicated to this service. I am happy to think that our two nations are today more closely linked than ever before by a common tradition of freedom and a common faith.

'While thoughts like these are passing through our minds we do not forget the men who brought this great ship into being. For them she must ever be a source of pride and, I am sure, of affection. I congratulate them warmly on the fruits of their labour. The launch of a ship is like the inception of all great human enterprises – an act of faith. We cannot foretell the future, but in preparing for it we must show our trust in a divine providence and in ourselves. We proclaim our belief that by the grace of God and by man's patience and goodwill order may yet be brought out of confusion, and peace out of turmoil. With that hope and prayer in our hearts, we send forth upon her mission this noble ship.'

But the launching ceremony that was being broadcast to the nation by radio did not go without incident.

The timber shoring, that had supported the liner's 40,000 ton launching weight during building, had been removed the day before the launch, lowering the liner onto the greased sliding ways. Only a few timbers remained in place and these would be knocked away shortly before the launch.

The hull of the ship that had been also specially stiffened internally by temporary wooden shores to strengthen her for what would possibly be the most critical journey of her career, was held in place by triggers. Her weight was now mainly supported by the heavily greased ways (the grease comprised ten tons of tallow and soft soap) with her bows cradled in a strong wood and steel support known as the fore-poppet.

Rams would be used to give the ship an initial push should she not gather sufficient momentum once the triggers had been remotely released from the launching platform. Conversely, to prevent the liner from gathering too much speed – and also to prevent her from ramming the opposite bank (should she veer from her astern course towards the specially dredged River Cart that joined the Clyde opposite to the yard) – eighteen bundles of chains would slow her progress. These bundles, of between 55 and 70 tons each, and totalling 2,350 tons, were secured to the ship's side by steel cables attached to eye bolts, and would be pulled into action to maintain the launch speed at a safe and manageable rate: the liner would reach a speed of 15 miles an hour during launch. Even these bundles of chains had historic maritime antecedents as some of them came from that daring (but at 16,000 tons far too big and advanced for her time) creation of Isambard Brunel – the *Great Eastern*.

As the moment arrived for the launch the *Queen Elizabeth* was delicately balanced on the ways and for many hours previously, because of the removal of most of the supporting timbers, an almost imperceptible movement had already taken place which would be magnified into magnificent action once the restraining triggers were released.

As Scotland's poet Robert Burns once wrote 'The best laid schemes o' mice an' men gang aft a-gley' so events in the shipyard almost took a different course to those planned.

After the formal speeches had been completed there was a pause as high tide was awaited. During the pause the Queen was presented with a sixteenth century inlaid casket from Saxony containing an album of photographs of the ship's building and the princesses played with a small model of the ship on her ways that had been used to explain the launching. Suddenly a crash of breaking timbers was heard and No. 552, on her own volition, started on her un-named journey towards the Clyde.

'She's away!'

At around the same time the Queen's microphone failed but, with great presence of mind, Her Majesty quietly and almost unheard by those around her said 'I name this ship *Queen Elizabeth* and wish success to her and all who sail in her.' Then, with the pair of gold scissors that Queen Mary had used to perform the launching ceremony of her namesake, she cut the red, white and blue ribbon which sent the bottle of Empire wine to break, just in time, against the liner's accelerating bow.

After the ceremony the Royal party departed but the other guests adjourned to the shipyard's Mould Loft (where more usually the lines of ships' frames were converted from scale drawings to faired, full size shapes on to a large floor. Wooden templates were then formed around these lines from which the steel frames etc were shaped) which had been specially laid out for the post-launch tea.

After almost launching herself the liner is sent down the ways to join her natural element for the first time.
Winchester Publications

During his speech Sir Percy Bates, chairman of the Cunard – White Star Line, recalled the circumstances in which the *Queen Elizabeth* – which was even now being towed and gently nudged into her fitting-out berth – and her elder sister, the superb *Queen Mary*, had come into being.

The liners were a result of Sir Percy's own initiative which was itself a fulfilment of a long cherished dream held by many ship owners: that a weekly transatlantic ferry service should be maintained by two ships rather than by the three, or even four, (sometimes mismatched) vessels that had previously – and expensively – maintained the same timetable.

As Sir Percy said in his speech,

'The ship you have just seen launched is no slavish copy of her sister. I described the sister, the *Queen Mary*, as the smallest and slowest ship that would do the job.' Sir Percy then briefly described the changes that made the *Elizabeth* an improvement on the *Queen Mary*: 'Naval architecture and marine engineering have not stood still since we contracted for 'No. 534' (the shipyard contract number of the *Queen Mary* by which she popularly known until the very moment of her launch) 'and we tried hard to make use of their progress to get the functional requirements for the sister ship expressed in a smaller hull. We found it impossible. For our schedule we need no more speed than the *Queen Mary* has got.' (The twenty-seven boilers in the *Queen Mary* had been reduced to twelve in the *Elizabeth* as one result of technological changes.)

Sir Percy elaborated: 'There is no sense in having one-half of a weekly service faster than the other. Yet technical advances made it absurd for us to repeat what we had done. There had to be changes. These changes have cost us little or no money. They can hardly be needed in speed, though I think 'No. 552' – the *Elizabeth* – 'might travel a little faster than 'No. 534', but they can be expressed in economy in the weekly job of crossing the Atlantic.'

The two *Queens* would also differ uniquely from their superliner contemporaries. 'Ships of State' of other lines, especially foreign, had been built with state aid and run with state subsidies. The *Queens* were different. They had been built with repayable loans and would run with great profit.

Meanwhile, as the tea progressed, the sparkling new *Queen Elizabeth* rested on the waters of the River Clyde, resplendent in her livery of white, black and red (strangely the same colours adopted by Hitler and his nefarious gang for the Nazi party which would soon so dramatically influence the Queen's career). But unbeknown to those present (or if they did foresee the future they did not voice their fears) it would be a long time before the *Queen Elizabeth* would become the ambassadress of the 'Noble Mission' of which the Queen had spoken.

Immediately after her launch the newly named *Queen Elizabeth* is taken to her fitting-out berth.

UCS Records/Glasgow University archives

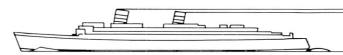

Chapter 2

Sisters, Not Twins

The idea that was to evolve into the *Queen Elizabeth* had been sketched out just over ten years previously, in 1926.

It was then that the original plans for her elder sister that was to become the *Queen Mary* were first quantified: the first vessel of the hitherto elusive two-ship North Atlantic express service.

Planning, preparation and building of the *Queen Mary*, the first of the giant thousand-foot liners (then popularly known solely by her shipyard number of '534') went bravely ahead. During the course of her construction the world was beset by the economic plague of the Great Depression. As a consequence of this, Cunard was forced to suspend work on the liner just before Christmas 1931.

The enormous, almost completed, hull of No. 534 had lain rusting on the stocks for over two years until the spring of 1934. By then the Labour Member of Parliament for Dumbarton Burghs, the Hon. David Kirkwood, aggrieved by the unemployment in his ship-yard constituency, had petitioned the Government for assistance to enable the Cunar-der to be completed, thus providing work for his constituents. This in turn would rekindle employment in the multitude of sub-contracting industries and spearhead Britain's recovery from years of financial limbo.

Kirkwood's appeal was heeded and the liner became a majestic and popular symbol of the British revival from the Depression as 'Bankies' (Clyde-bankers) marched triumphantly back to work on 3rd April 1934.

Work on the ship began with clearing tons of rust and thousands of birds' nests that had accumulated over the months of idleness in readiness for the construction to restart.

For its part in this daring rescue package the Government had agreed to advance Cunard a total of £9.5 million (1938 value) on condition that the Cunard merge with the famous, but ailing, White Star Line.

The advance was broken down into three parts, the first of which was a payment of £3 million to complete '534'. Secondly, £1.5 million was to be provided as working capital for the newly formed company of Cunard – White Star Limited which would manage the new ship and the combined fleets and, thirdly, a loan of £5 million would be made available, when requested, for a sister to 'No 534'.

Surrounded by a eulogizing publicity campaign that satiated the public's appetite for superlatives, details and the promise of the grandeur to come (everything, it seemed, except for the actual name of the liner) No. 534 blossomed into completion, towering above the smokey, revitalized town that was giving her life.

Finally, on a rainy 26th September 1936, their Majesties King George V and his consort, Queen Mary, came to Scotland to launch the 1019 foot liner.

After the King's speech, during which he magnificently described the liner being launched as 'the stateliest ship now in being', the Queen cut a ribbon (using a pair of gold scissors which would be used in two later launches of regal Cunard liners) that sent a bottle of wine crashing against the ship's bow, naming the liner after herself – *Queen Mary*.

A few months previously, in February 1936, a preliminary announcement was made of Cunard's intention to build a sister to the ship then currently building on Clydeside. But not until the promised money had been obtained from the Government would a builder be selected and the *Queen Mary*'s performance – and that of her competition – studied in detail.

The *Mary* sailed on her glittering maiden voyage on 27th May 1936, surrounded by a blaze of well-earned publicity. This had been preceded by a triumphant cruise off the southern coast of Britain, providing the population with a splendid view of the new ship whilst giving members of the various sub-contractors a memorable cruise by way of thanking them for their hard work.

Shortly after the *Mary*'s entrance into service she soon disproved some of the optimistic theories that had accompanied her building.

Being over a thousand feet long it was anticipated that she would be steady on even the longest Atlantic swell – but she still rolled miserably in rough weather.

Fleets of ambulances would sometimes meet the berthing liner at Southampton or in New York to take off

An impressive view of the *Queen Elizabeth*'s elder sister, the *Queen Mary*, on speed trials off Arran.
'Wonderful Story of the Sea'

The magnificent but revolutionary French liner *Normandie* seen here tendering at Spithead. It was the clean upperdecks of this liner that influenced the design of the *Queen Elizabeth*.　　　　*Red Funnel Group, Southampton*

people injured during rough crossings. Handrails were hurriedly installed (these had been omitted due to the faith put in her stability) and during her first winter refit she underwent an enormous internal rebuild with additional stiffening added in critical areas.

She emerged a steadier ship but she would still continue to roll, particularly with a following sea even after leaving rough weather well astern. Her crew said that 'she could roll the milk out of a cup of tea!'

She was, nevertheless, a supremely popular ship right from the outset, continuing to command the interest that had been afforded her during her construction. Royal visits undertaken by the Prince of Wales at Clydebank and by Queen Mary and members of the Royal Family shortly after the liner's arrival at Southampton, all helped to build up the fervour of excitement prior to the *Queen Mary*'s introduction into service.

The maiden voyage was broadcast to eager radio listeners all over the British Empire with, amongst other attractions, Henry Hall and his Orchestra playing the specially composed 'Somewhere at Sea' at all hours of the day to suit tea-times all over the world.

Cunard approached the Government, then represented by the Chancellor of the Exchequer Neville Chamberlain, and asked for the release of the third part of the promised loan for its intended purpose: the financing of the second of the two intended thousand foot liners, anticipated since the keel laying of the *Queen Mary*.

In the second half of June 1936 in reply to a question in the House of Commons, the Chancellor said 'I have received a reply from the Cunard–White Star Company for authority to use the sum available under the North Atlantic Shipping Act for the construction of a sister ship .... I have agreed in principle.' The Chancellor added that Cunard had received preliminary tenders from various yards and were negotiating in the first instance with John Brown and Company as they had a slip that was almost ready for the work, other than adding or replacing piling to the existing No. 4 slip, and their experience in building giant liners was second to none.

The Financial Secretary to the treasury, Herbert Morrison, made an announcement in the House on Tuesday 28th July to the effect that the Chancellor had given his final assent to the money being released after receiving ample evidence from Cunard that their choice of yard had been the correct one.

A little while previously and perhaps as an inducement to Cunard, Lord Aberconway, chairman of John Brown's

Clydebank shipyard, said that if his yard were entrusted with the work they would hope to build an even better ship than the *Queen Mary*, of which they were all proud.

The Scottish yard had apparently been Cunard's choice from the start as Sir Percy Bates had privately intimated as much to Lord Aberconway at the launch of the *Queen Mary*.

The contract was signed on October 6th 1936.

Cunard was determined that their new ship would not be an evolutionary development of previous ships – as the *Mary* had been – but would be based on the latest revolutionary developments that had taken place in naval architecture and marine engineering.

To this end Sir Percy Bates would not be rushed. As he had said in his post launch speech, after the *Elizabeth* had been offered to the elements, that she would be '..... no slavish copy of her sister.' And to achieve this Cunard had looked elsewhere for inspiration other than relying wholly on their own experience, invaluable, though, that this had been.

And what better ship to study than the *Queen Mary*'s arch-rival in the North Atlantic stakes – the French Line's superb *Normandie*? After all, the two ships had been carrying on a contest as to which was the larger and the faster. To obtain first-hand observations of the French ship, Cunard booked passage for one of their designers who travelled as a grocer! Taking care not to ask too many technical questions that would expose his assumed identity, the information that he obtained proved to be of great use in the design of the new ship. Various structural changes had been effected on both the *Normandie* and the *Queen Mary* since their introduction into service and a rivalry existed to prove each ship the faster. Cunard, of course, denied that there was any rivalry on their part to gain the speed record, saying that any attempt to do so was merely to gather information needed for the design of the *Mary*'s forthcoming partner.

However, the two companies did have a sensible working arrangement whereby it was ensured that their sailings were alternated. The *Queen Mary* was also running a weekly service with her elder cousin, the four funnelled *Aquitania*. As a result, the latter ship was hard pressed, her turn-round times in the terminal ports being reduced to a minimum in order to maintain her half of the service.

The *Normandie* had one edge on the *Queen Mary* in being aesthetically more pleasing to the eye through her revolutionary streamlining and lack of visible deck 'clutter'. Costing almost twice as much as the *Mary*, the French liner was perhaps also that more lavish in her first class appointments.

But the *Mary* had a slightly better hull and the two ships vied with each other to achieve the cream-of-the-trade appeal of being the fastest afloat.

For two years the competition raged, with the honours passing to and fro. Structural changes helped to reduce the effects of vibration in both ships as did improvements to propulsion systems which honed up speeds by valuable fractions of a knot.

As a triumphant fanfare to the launch of the *Queen Elizabeth* the *Mary* captured the Blue Ribband – although

Cunard refused to acknowledge the recently introduced Hale's Trophy as a tangible symbol of their achievement – in August 1938 with a speed of 31.69 knots, a record that would stand for 14 years.

Sir Percy Bates was determined that the *Elizabeth* would be able to exceed her sister's performance but sensibly refuted the suggestion that the two ships would compete with each other. This would be expensive as well as nonsensical.

For many years warships of His Majesty's Royal Navy had used watertube boilers of the Yarrow design to give them short bursts of high speed. This design had been bravely adopted for the *Mary* where sustained, all-year-round high speed was required to maintain her timetable and to ensure that a reserve of power would be available to make up time lost during adverse weather conditions.

Sir Percy had also wisely waited for other anticipated improvements in boiler design to occur. As a result only twelve boilers would be placed in the *Queen Elizabeth* rather than the twenty four that the *Mary* needed to raise the same amount of steam in order to produce the same amount of power.

The reduction in boiler room space had several follow-on effects. A smaller boiler room resulted in more space being made for additional passengers (crew numbers were also increased to cater for these); two funnels were erected instead of the three as on the older ship and were self-supporting, having their stays on the inside of the stack, thus taking up less passenger deck space; fans of a newer design were also mounted inside the ship giving the new liner a cleaner, uncluttered upper deck. The prominent square ventilation cowls on the *Mary* were also dispensed with on the new ship.

Another obvious difference between the two ships was the lack of a forward well deck on the younger liner. This had been included on the *Mary* to spend the force of any heavy sea that might break over her bow before the water could damage the superstructure front. This anticipated event had never occurred and was considered very unlikely to occur, so the well-space area was plated in and used for additional revenue.

The bow, unlike that of the *Mary*, was heavily raked. This enabled a third anchor, the bower, to be carried allowing the anchor to fall well clear of the stem; it also made it possible for the ship to ride at anchor without the problem of the anchor cable chaffing the stem plates when the ship swung due to changes in wind and tide.

The rake also gave the *Elizabeth* a longer overall length: 1,031 feet as against the 1,019.5 feet of the *Mary*.

So gradually designs were completed and approved, orders for steel plate, machinery and a host of items for kitchens, restaurants, cabins, lounges, etc., were placed and on Friday 4th December 1936, without ceremony, the keel of No. 552 was laid.

Sir Percy would later describe the giant liner as '.... human audacity in steel.' But on the European continent the evil power of Adolf Hitler grew concurrently with the new liner. This human audacity in terror would eventually rob the new *Queen* of her youth.

Chapter Three

The Making Of A Queen

It was almost a foregone conclusion that the two Cunard liners would be the queens of the Atlantic. With the *Queen Mary* already in service it was popularly assumed, even before Her Majesty the Queen gave her royal assent to do so in February 1938, that Shipyard Number 552 would become the *Queen Elizabeth*. The liner thus, if unofficially, had a name by which she could be known during the course of her building. In contrast Number 534 had not become the *Queen Mary* until the very moment of her launch.

With the keel of No. 552 laid on slip No. 4 and construction proceeding beyond the laying of the keel plates and the erection of vertical keel, floors, tank tops and frame legs etc. (all carried out by shipwrights – 'The Shipbuilders'), other trades moved in to make a start on the outfit of the gradually rising shell. Pipework for steam, oil and water; electric cable runs; ventilation and air-conditioning trunking runs were 'lined-off', their locations being marked in thin, white paint lines.

Employment once again rose in the shipyard as materials arrived for forming.

Drawings for the ship had been transferred from their scaled paper conceptions to full sized curves on the mould-loft (or scrieve board) floor, their graceful shapes being etched (scrieved) into the giant black board-like floor. From these curves, 'faired' to perfection, the steelworkers would make templates which would then be used as a guide when hot steel sections were hammered into shape to become the frames of the ship.

As these frames were erected, reaching upwards like out-stretched giant fingers cupped to catch the sky, so transverse beams joined opposite frames to provide the supports for deck plates, pillars connected beams of one deck to those of the deck above to provide support and strength.

A week before keel laying the last few timbers are laid on slip No. 4. The wooden building blocks would eventually have to support 40,000 tons of steel.

UCS Records/ Glasgow University Archives

Other templates of wooden battens were taken from the erected frames and, using these, huge steel plates were cut, shaped and drilled with rows of holes corresponding with lines of rivet holes drilled into the frames.

The plates were then offered into position and bolted through an occasional hole to hold the plates temporarily in place whilst riveters fastened the plate permanently into place. The noise of their rivet guns sent their familiar staccato rhythms, typical of pre-war shipyards everywhere, over the yard's walls into the town and surrounding countryside. By their noise the rivet guns told all and sundry that employment was once again in the proud Scottish town which was now building the largest liner that the world had ever seen.

The lesser sound of caulking guns would also be heard as the edges of adjoining plates were caulked to ensure watertightness.

But it was not only in Clydebank that No. 552 brought employment and prosperity. Many of the products that would be built into or used on the new Cunard liner would either be of United Kingdom manufacture or come from one of the various globe-scattered countries that constituted the British Empire.

From Glasgow and all over the British Isles came huge castings for propeller brackets along with stern, bow and hawse-pipe castings, four 32-ton manganese bronze propellers, steel plates and sections of various shapes, machinery, electrical generators and switchboards, four anchors at 16½ tons apiece, a 140 ton rudder with its own inspection door, ten million rivets, twenty-six lifeboats and their motors, two thousand portholes, twelve water tube

Above: Watched by two bowler-hatted managers, the first keel plates of 'No. 552' are laid on Friday 4th December 1936. *UCS Records/Glasgow University Archives*

Right: Supported by timber shoring the framework of the after double bottom tanks begin to show the fine lines of the liner's hull.
UCS Records/ Glasgow University Archives

Above: Almost nine months after the laying of the keel plates the side frames of No. 552 veer up from the slip. The bridge in the foreground was originally constructed over the shipyard railway to support the bow of the *Queen Mary* during her construction.
UCS Records/Glasgow University Archives

Left: As the erection of frames is completed shipwrights and rivetters fit the shell plates to the skeleton of the ship. This midship section shows the plating method adopted.
Stewart Bale Ltd/Queen Elizabeth Historical Society

The strengthened brackets for the inner propeller make an impressive sight.

Stewart Bale Ltd/Queen Elizabeth Historical Society

This photograph clearly shows the bridge built over the ship-yard railway. A locomotive whistles a warning as it prepares to pass under the liners bow.

Stewart Bale Ltd/Queen Elizabeth Historical Society

An hydraulic riveting machine makes life a little easier for the contemporary workmen. March 1938.

UCS Records/Glasgow University Archives

boilers, fans, navigational aids, glass, silver-ware, carpets, curtains, chairs, tables – the list was almost endless. The weight of steel in the hull and machinery alone would be in the region of 50,000 tons.

Items, such as much of the machinery, would come from John Brown's own works and from the area around Glasgow but many contractors and sub-contractors were huddled around Manchester, Birmingham, Sheffield and London.

From Dundee in the north to Belfast in the west; from Norwich and Ipswich in the east to Cowes and Fowey in the south, the British Isles produced the essential items that eventually found their ways converging through the gates of John Brown and Company, Shipbuilders.

Apart from the leather from a thousand hides of cattle that became furnishings and wall panels, and the use of satins for decorative, quilted wall-padding, the most exotic-ally sounding of the decorative – as well as practical in some cases – materials were, as on the *Mary*, provided by the woods used on board.

Dozens of exotic, rare and unusual timbers were used as either decking, bulkhead linings in public rooms and first-class cabins, in furniture or for the revitalized art of marquetry. Fine examples of the latter art would be found in the more expensive cabins and in the public rooms of all classes.

These woods came from all over the Empire and some would be used solely in a large piece of marquetry that would hang (in pre-war days) in the Main Lounge.

This piece of woodwork combined the skills and art of the designer with those of the woodworker. Entitled 'The Canterbury Tales', it had been designed by George Ramon

13

Above: By the beginning of April 1938 much of the hull steelwork is complete. The men standing on the after structure are dwarfed by the construction work surrounding them.

UCS Records/Glasgow University Archives

Left: Looking forward, the bare frames and deck beams contrast starkly with the deck plates being fitted in the foreground.

UCS Records/Glasgow University Archives

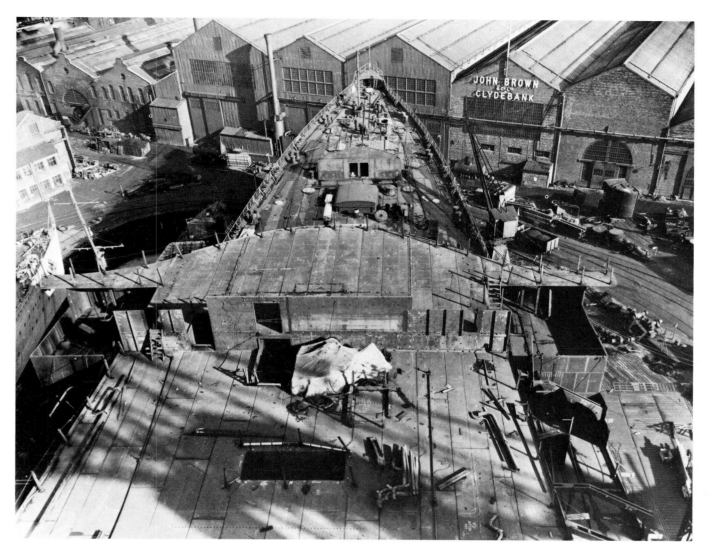

Above: With the construction of the bridge underway the bow of 'No. 552' points proudly towards the workshops that are bringing her into being. The bow of the submarine depot ship, HMS *Maidstone*, can be seen to the left of the photograph.
Stewart Bale Ltd/Queen Elizabeth Historical Society

Right: By the end of August 1938 the propeller cones (or bosses) are ready to be bolted into position onto one of the port propellers. *UCS Records/Glasgow University Archives*

in response to a call for something that typically depicted Britain (he originally thought of 'Fog'!); the work was executed by A.T. Dunn and family.

Woods used on and in the ship included London Plane, Scottish Pine and blackened, centuries-old 'Bog Oak' (retrieved from the peat bogs of Ireland). Also from Britain came Sycamore, Laburnum, Acacia and Wych Elm.

From the forests of the Dominion of Canada came Birch and Blistered – and Bird's Eye Maples. From Australia came Silky Oak and the native Bean Wood. A thousand tons of Burma Teak was used as deck cladding and for other carpentry work. Laurelwood, Coralwood and

Above: As the painting of the hull reaches completion so the scaffolding is taken down. The upper superstructure can be painted later using platforms slung from the upper deck.
Stewart Bale Ltd/Queen Elizabeth Historical Society

Left: A view from amidships looking aft shows the completed hull of 'No. 552' free of scaffolding and with work continuing on the superstructure.
Stewart Bale Ltd/Queen Elizabeth Historical Society

Left: Yet without the letters that will make up the liner's name and part of registry, the stern of the *Queen Elizabeth* looms above the launching ways. Old car tyres protect the sensitive edges of the enormous propellers.
Stewart Bale Ltd/Queen Elizabeth Historical Society

Above: The balanced rudder (with its bolted access hatch) and a tyre-protected propeller flanked the carefully painted draught marks. *Stewart Bale Ltd/Queen Elizabeth Historical Society*

Prima Vera came to grace the ship. Cherry was used in many fine carvings.

From North and South America, from French Guiana, the Indies and Scandinavia came Satina, Sandalwoods and Coromandel; black and figured Ebonies, Thuya, Mahoganies and Zebrano, Rosewood, Purple Heart, Almond and the curious sounding Colo Bolo. Lignum Vitae (black and yellow and denser than water), Tulipwood, Beefwood, Olivewood and Walnut; scented Camphor, Orange and Palm. The galleys of old never carried a richer cargo.

From the Palace at Hampton Court came a Virginia Creeper that was 120 years old; perhaps, most romantic of all there was the 'Waterloo Elm'. The veneer of this lined the Captain's cabin and was, in fact, Wych Elm that had been used as piling under the Waterloo Bridge of 1811. Bleached grey by water and time it had been removed from its position in 1936 and a small brass plaque was placed in its final resting place to record its pedigree.

Lower class accommodation and crews' quarters were generally lined with enamel-painted plywood, ⅝ inch thick.

As the ship grew upwards in stature from the building blocks so more men were taken on at the shipyard, finding employment in the various outfitting trades.

After the *Queen Mary* had been launched many men had been saved from unemployment by the contract awarded to their yard to build the Royal Naval submarine dept ship HMS *Maidstone*. Not only did the construction of this ship keep many skilled men on the payroll until No. 552 was ready for building, but the launching of the naval ship served as a scaled experiment for the launch of its

larger merchant sister. Amongst other information gleaned the pressures on its hull during launch provided much important data.

The giant liner was constructed on No. 4 slip by using (quite astoundingly, looking back now over half-a-century) 5 ton derrick cranes and a 10 ton tower crane that had been erected at the forward end of the slip for the construction of the *Mary*. Heavy castings were erected by using derrick poles or sheer legs.

Steam locomotives would deliver steel plates loaded on low wagons to the building slip but lighter items such as pipes, ventilation trunking, timber etc. were brought by horse-drawn lorries. The horses belonged to a local haulier who stabled them across the road from the shipyard. Careful, painstaking and satisfyingly creative work was being carried on, it seemed, to the patient beat of horses' hooves.

To ensure that good progress was maintained during construction the General and Shipyard Managers met all the various departmental head foremen at the gangway every Friday.

This 'Glee Party' – as it was known to the men – then toured the vessel deck by deck. Any problems that were encountered were resolved by the foremen concerned by sending in extra men to assist temporarily with the work that had fallen behind and bring the construction plan back to its timetable.

Very little overtime was worked on the ship before launch. Sam Campbell, a joiner who had worked on the outfit of both *Queens*, recalls that a skilled craftsman received £3.2s.0d (£3.10) for a 47 hour week, although

Supported by wooden shores (most of which would be knocked away a day before the launch) and flanked by the 5-ton gantry cranes the hull dwarfs the shipyard around it. *Stewart Bale Ltd/Queen Elizabeth Historical Society*

such apparent occasion occurred in mid-1939 when a two week demarcation strike was held by 350 plumbers who walked out in protest at a claimed encroachment on their field of work by coppersmiths; the plumbers claimed that the copper piping being used by the coppersmiths came under their jurisdiction.

By the time that her launch day arrived the *Queen Elizabeth* had a weight on the slip of 39,400 tons. She measured 1,031 feet in overall length, had a waterline length of 1,004 feet and was 965 feet between perpendiculars. Moulded breadth, measured to the inside of the shell plating (or outside face of frames), was 118 feet. The liner stood 132 feet from her keel to the top of her superstructure and her Promenade Deck was 724 feet in length. Her hull, embracing fourteen decks, would have a draught of 39 feet 6½ inches once finished and stored for sea.

The public had already had a chance to see what the new liner would look like once completed as an eighteen foot model of the ship had been on display at the Empire Exhibition in Glasgow opened a year before the launch.

On the day of the launch the Royal party visited the Exhibition before going on to the shipyard and Princess Elizabeth became the Exhibition's millionth visitor.

After her launch the liner was towed to her fitting-out berth. A barrier was then constructed around the ship to shut her off from the river. This was to prevent Clyde-borne silt building-up around and under the vessel thus making her a grounded prisoner even before her first voyage.

the steelworking trades made this up to £4 per week by piecework.

As an indication of the worsening European situation the keel of the Royal Navy's newest battleship, HMS *Duke of York*, was laid on 5th May 1937, on the adjoining slip to the rapidly growing liner.

The building of the warship would decrease the number of spectators (attending the launching of the Cunarder) who could be accommodated on the starboard side of the slipway. To overcome this, extra stands were built on the west side of the fitting-out basin. An estimated 250,000 would attend the launch with stands, enclosures and special steamers being used as vantage points.

Fortunately very little industrial unrest was encountered during the building and fitting-out. The only

For almost five years the shipyard had carried on a correspondence with the Clyde Navigation Trust, dealing with the safe navigation of the liner on her one and only journey to the open sea.

This would involve a great deal of dredging and the removal of rock outcrops that might hazard the ship's safe progress. The river was also widened in places, especially at Dalmuir. It was here that the *Queen Mary*, caught by a gust of wind on her journey downriver from the shipyard, swivelled about and temporarily ran aground for many anxious seconds that could have proved disastrous for both ship and for future river traffic.

Meanwhile, however, the *Elizabeth* lay alongside her jetty, cosseted with careful attention that would make her the new sovereign of the sea.

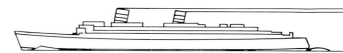

Chapter Four

Flight Of An Empress

During the fourteen months that followed her launch the interior and exterior of the *Queen Elizabeth* steadily approached completion.

Large windows that would give panoramic views of the passing ocean were cut into the steel plating along the Promenade Deck and into the gracefully stepped curves of the superstructure front. These areas had been left as uncut steel structures in order to maintain strength and stiffness along the upper part of the ship during the brief, critical moments of the launch.

The *Queen* took on her identity as the letters of her name were fixed on either side of her bow and, also along with 'Liverpool' as her port of registry, on the upper part of her black hull around the stern.

The letters at her bow were each two and a half feet high and the name *Queen Elizabeth* occupied a length of nearly sixty-eight feet.

In overall charge of the vessel's interior decoration was G. Gray Wornum and within his sphere of supervision came the artistic talents of many people whose works would be on display in many of the better cabins as well as in the thirty-seven public rooms of all classes.

In the space of this book it is only possible to describe a few of these rooms with an emphasis on the Cabin Class, renamed First Class in post-war days.

The large and airy Main Lounge, on the Promenade Deck, in which hung George Ramon's 'Canterbury Tales' marquetry, was panelled with a tawny pink Canadian maple burr veneer. The wood was put into relief by other panels covered in leather of light grey, pale blue and buff. Aft (portside) of this room was a writing room, the alcoves of which were also lined with leather.

Two fine paintings ('Elsinore' and 'Dover Harbour') by Norman Wilkinson, the famous marine artist, were displayed in the Main Lounge and these would be hung in place the day before the liner left Clydebank by joiner Sam Campbell.

The carpet in the lounge represented a broad swirl of rope (a theme often repeated in the ship's decor) woven in tan on a darker background.

The restaurants of the three classes were placed on the same deck, interspaced with the appropriate kitchens, and thus named the deck on which they were situated (Restaurant Deck).

Snug alongside her fitting-out berth the *Queen* is kept company by two warships. The launch of the submarine depot ship HMS *Maidstone* (right) provided much valuable data for the launch of the giant Cunarder. *UCS Records/Glasgow University Archives*

This needlework tapestry designed by Miss E. Esmonde-White, assisted by Mr Leroux S. Leroux, was destined to be hung in the Main Restaurant.   *Southampton City Museums*

The Cabin (First) Class Restaurant was carpeted with a shadowed hexagonal pattern weave and over the room's entrance hung the royal cypher carved in lime by Bainbridge Copnall. The Queen had requested that a portrait of her should not be hung in the ship so, as a compensation, her coat of arms with its three lions and three bows (representing the family arms of Bowes-Lyon) was suggested in lieu.

The main dining room of the Restaurant was one hundred and ten feet long by one hundred and fifteen feet wide and was panelled in myrtle cluster.

Above an alcove was set a clock, the numbers being represented by radial dashes. Next to each of these dashes was a beautifully carved sign of the Zodiac, again carved by Bainbridge Copnall, giving a garland effect.

On another wall hung a tapestry depicting Venus in the waves with four large sea-horses and three 'mer-children' in front of her. The tapestry, although woven in England, was the work of two South African designers – Miss Eleanor Esmonde-White and Mr Leroux Smith-Leroux.

Having its own kitchen and perhaps the most exclusive room on board, the Verandah Grill was decorated in ivory coloured veneers and peach coloured velvet curtains. Confronted by a small dance floor – for those who liked to dance as well as dine – a small stage stood against the forward bulkhead of the room.

The daytime sea views obtained from the grill (other than for when it was foggy!) proved a great attraction to those who were willing to pay an extra charge for the privilege of dining in the grill. Cunard would capitalise on this asset when, almost thirty years later, their second ship to be named after the Queen Mother (as Queen Elizabeth would become) had all her restaurants built into the higher

The First Class Observation Lounge and Cocktail Bar as it would later appear.   *Southampton City Museums*

The centre portion of the First Class Main Restaurant as furnished in post-war years.   *Southampton City Museums*

As the ship is gradually fitted out so she assumes the fittings of luxury. The Ballroom here is almost complete.
UCS Records/Glasgow University Archives

Miss Esmonde-White's large tapestry hangs in-situ in the Main Restaurant, as yet not fitted with tables or chairs. This and other interior photographs following were taken on the liner's arrival in New York, March 1940.

UCS Records/Glasgow University Archives

A Third Class cabin with twin bunks as completed.

UCS Records/Glasgow University Archives

Part of the Cabin (First) Class Gymnasium.

UCS Records/Glasgow University Archives

sections of the ship; an advantage also made possible by built-in stabilisers.

The other restaurants on R Deck were sited low in the *Lizzie* as it was expected that any untoward motion would be least felt there, an assumption soon upset by the tables left unoccupied during rough weather.

The Smoke Room was described as '.... magnificent .... with its atmosphere of quiet dignity'. The four distinct

Above: The beautiful wood veneers in the Cabin (First) Class Library can be seen here to full advantage.
The University Archives, the University of Liverpool

Right: Tourist/3rd Class Dining Room (photographed in New York April 1940).
UCS Records/Glasgow University Archives

veneers were all cut from one giant walnut tree that had grown in the Isle of Wight.

Above the triple electric fireplace in this room was a series of bas-reliefs, one placed on each of nine veneered panels. The reliefs were individually carved or cast from the principle materials used in the building of the liner – lead, glass, white metal, steel, wood, rubber, aluminium, bronze and copper – each one cleverly represented the source, production or abstract spirit of the material presented.

Carvings representing Hunting, Shooting and Fishing as well as a clock were displayed in the Smoke Room, all carved by Dennis Dunlop. A map, designed by Macdonald Gill, occupied another bulk-head. Models of the two *Queens* were supposed to move on this map to reflect the relative positions of the two ships at all times of the day. The carpet contained both the colours of the Cunard Line and of the sea, all set against a tawny background. Armchairs were in light cobalt blue and fawn. Outboard on either side of the Smoke Room was a garden lounge both of which had direct sea views.

The Salon, also on the Promenade Deck, with walls of quilted satin and a gilded ceiling was used as a perfect setting for dances. Opposite to the stage a deep recess contained a lively jungle scene of tropical birds, antelope and monkeys. Designed by another South African, Jan Juta, the work had been executed by Fred Barker in painted glass and enamel. Twelve panels of fish carved in wood and covered in silver foil completed the decor.

The cinema/theatre could be used by Tourist as well as by Cabin Class (Third Class had their own). Seating three hundred and thirty eight the room suggested the national colours of those three nations between whose ports of Southampton, Cherbourg and New York the Queen would travel. A blue carpet, furnishings of vermilion and walls of ivory white presented a very comfortable room.

The two higher classes each had its own swimming pool but Cabin Class was the only class to have a dedicated library – Tourist for instance had to make do with a few bookshelves in their lounge – but four thousand volumes in total were carried on board.

Forward of the Main Lounge was the Main Entrance Hall, both rooms extending over the width of the superstructure. In the entrance hall w as a bronze statue of a female figure swimming through the arms of her male companion, both figures surrounded by dolphins: the whole seeming to balance on one leg of the male figure.

Inspired by the music of Sibelius and entitled 'Oceanides' the piece had been sculpted by Maurice Lambert and was not originally intended for the ship – George Ramon had seen it in the artist's studio during a visit and had subsequently asked Sir Percy Bates to come along and view it. Sir Percy was impressed (which was more than he was when he recommended that some paintings intended for the *Queen Mary* should be given to a blind home!) and the work was purchased.

The forward port of the Promenade Deck housed the Observation Lounge and Cocktail Bar. Set in the forward curvature of the superstructure the lounge had forward views over the bow to the seas rushing towards the ship.

Panelled in sycamore that had been dyed lobster red, the lounge contained more George Ramon marquetry, this time of circus scenes. At the after end of the lounge was a cocktail bar panelled in silver Sycamore studded with metal stars.

It should be finally noted that the public rooms of the Tourist and Third Classes, although not so sumptuous as those in Cabin, were light, spacious and well-appointed. The Winter Gardens in Third were particularly delightful. Fresh enamel paint, an occasional hint of highly polished veneer and a variety of plants gave the room an airy appearance. Placed in the lowest superstructure deck forward it had its own promenade on the fore deck of the ship.

When considering the comfort of those on board the Company had decided against the installation of stabilisers. The Times said in their special 'Cunard – White Star Supplement' of Tuesday 27th September 1938, that '... no practicable installation of this type '(ie gyro-stabilizers)' could possibly be of the slightest use in vessels of the size of the *Queen Mary* and *Queen Elizabeth* .... to date the safest and easiest crossings are secured by sheer size and huge transverse inertia, coupled with a good form design, bilge keels of practicable dimensions and careful experienced seamanship. The stability of the *Queen Mary* has proved ample at all times to make the ship as safe and comfortable as it is possible for any vessel to be when passing through an Atlantic storm'.

Cunard and The Times had obviously temporarily forgotten the devastation on board the *Mary* caused by stormy weather when crockery and limbs alike had been broken and fleets of ambulances had met the ship on arrival!

But all this luxury (along with 3,603 people) had to be propelled across the North Atlantic at an average speed of 29.5 knots if the *Queen Elizabeth* were to maintain her half of the express weekly schedule.

To do this twelve Yarrow-type high pressure water tube boilers were built into four boiler rooms. In the *Mary* twenty four boilers had been equally divided in four boiler rooms (two rows of three placed athwartships in each) with three Scotch boilers in their own compartment, providing steam for the ship's hotel services.

However, the oil-burning boilers in the *Elizabeth* were to be sited only two abreast. Four of the boilers (two on No. 1 and two in No. 3 boiler rooms) were fitted with desuperheaters and reducing valves to provide steam for the hotel and in-port services, thus doing away with the need for dedicated boilers as on the *Mary*.

Two boilers were placed in Nos. 1 and 4 boiler rooms with four apiece in Nos. 2 and 3. Two compartments, containing air-conditioning plant, electrical generating plant and water-softening equipment, separated Nos. 2 and 3 boiler rooms.

The boilers, the largest such marine installations ever built, were constructed under licence by John Brown and Co. They each had a combustion chamber volume of 3,220 cubic feet; a steam generating surface of 20,530 square feet; a superstructure surface of 10,120 square feet; air pre-heating surface area of 27,300 square feet and produced a working pressure of 425 pounds per square inch (400 on the *Mary*) at a final steam temperature of 750 degrees

Photographed in July 1938 this picture shows the lower part of the forward funnel in position atop a ventilation intake. The design of these intakes (inspired by the *Normandie*) ridded the liner of the upper deck clutter of the *Queen Mary*'s square cowls.

UCS Records/Glasgow University Archives

Fahrenheit, 50 degrees more than the *Queen Mary*.

Because of the larger boiler units it was felt certain that the *Elizabeth* would prove to be more successful and economical than the *Mary*.

The steam from the boilers fed into four Parsons single reduction geared turbine engines placed two each in the forward and after engine rooms, astern of No. 4 boiler room. The two engines in the forward room drove the two outer propellers whilst the inner propellers were powered by the after engine room.

Each engine consisted of one high-, two intermediate-, and one low-pressure turbine, the steam from which exhausted into a condenser where it was cooled back into re-usable water.

The total output of the engines, each of which could be used independently, was 160,000 s.h.p. (shaft horse power).

Electricity came from four 2,200 kilowatt turbogenerators at 250 volts. These, along with four main and forty-three auxiliary switchboards produced enough power to light 30,000 lamps through 4,000 miles of wiring; operate 700 electric clocks; 800 telephones; drive 21 lifts (11 for passenger use and 10 for stores and services); keep 43,000 cubic feet of cold storage space suitable for meat, fish, fruit, vegetables, dairy produce, wines, beer, etc; and power kitchen machinery such as the potato peelers, meat mincers and choppers, raisin stoners, ice-breakers, fruit juice extractors, silver burnishers, dish washers, etc etc; and operate the 38 watertight doors in an emergency as well as keeping the 26 lifeboat motors ready warmed. Many improvements were made on the *Queen Elizabeth* from lessons learnt on her elder sister. For example, the engineers had originally been quartered near the engine rooms on the *Mary* but soon special quarters were built for them atop the Verandah Grill at the aft end of the superstructure. The *Lizzie* had custom-built accommodation for the engine room department, complete with ward room, forward of the Veranda Grill on the Sun Deck.

Whilst all this grandeur, power and luxury was being created on Clydeside the European situation gradually worsened.

Men and materials were taken away from the liner as Admiralty work took priority and the pace of work on board slowed down.

On 22nd August 1939 it was announced that the maiden voyage of the *Queen Elizabeth* was intended to

At noon on 16th November 1939 (a month after the outbreak of World War II) the first lighting of a boiler is undertaken.   *UCS Records/Glasgow University Archives*

commence on 24th April 1940. However, after war was declared between Great Britain and Germany on 3rd September 1939 and work slowed on the mighty Cunarder, the date of the anticipated maiden voyage became doubtful.

Questions were asked in Parliament as to what possible use the two vulnerable Cunard leviathans could be in wartime. Suggestions extended from laying-up the *Elizabeth* in a sheltered loch to selling her to the Americans; from converting her to an aircraft carrier-cum-plane transport (for which plans were later drawn up showing a cut-down superstructure and only one funnel forward and placed to starboard) to converting her to a cargo ship. The two ships' real potential had not yet been realised.

Churchill, still First Lord of the Admiralty, expressed his fears on the safety of the *Elizabeth*.

The *Queen Mary* was by now laid-up in New York having reached there on Monday September 4th, the day after war was declared, and Churchill feared that the still completing *Elizabeth* would fall victim to Nazi bombers. On 6th February, he ordered that the *Elizabeth* ' ... should keep away from the British Isles ...'.

Consequently a special licence was granted in early November for the supply of valuable steel and labour to complete the liner. This would allow work to progress sufficiently to enable her to sail to somewhere safe, wherever that was.

Also, the liner's fitting out berth would soon be needed for the battleship *Duke of York*, due to be launched on the 16th September 1939.

On the same day the last section of the liner's 44 x 29 foot elliptical, 80 and 78 foot high funnels was lifted into position. The two funnels (the forward taking the gases from 1 and 2 boiler rooms, the after one taking the rest) were self-supporting having not the external steel wire rope guys of the *Mary* but internal cross-rod bracing tie bars. Steam pipes were also carried internally to the three whistles (one aft, two forward).

These one-ton whistles were toned 'two octaves below middle A' and the deep, rich, glorious sound that bellowed forth would never cease to thrill – even ten miles away! Pulses from the melodious, vibrating roar could be felt up to twenty miles from the ship.

The ship was practically mechanically complete when ten days later, at noon on the 16th, a light smoke curled upwards from the funnels as the boilers were lit for the first time. In December, two days before the end of the old year, the engines were turned under steam.

Bollard and other tests could now be carried out on the engines of the stationary ship. Three months later the vessel was ready to sail for, it was rumoured, Southampton, the only British port with a dry-dock large enough to take the *Queens*.

The Luftwaffe learnt of these arrangements, which were supported by the arrival of crates of equipment in the Hampshire port marked with the ship's name and the forward booking of local hotel rooms for shipyard personnel, and they planned a warm reception for the liner.

His Majesty the King, accompanied by his wife, finally managed to visit the liner when he visited the shipyard to launch the *Duke of York* (his title before he became King) on 16th September 1939.

Monday 26th February was a dull, misty day and not many people saw the giantess slip from her berth and head down river.

The *Queen* was about to make her debut in history.

Chapter Five

"The Furye Of Her Enemies"

At the time of the *Queen Elizabeth*'s launch a letter to the London Times quoted a passage written four centuries before:

'The ship called the *Elizabeth Jonas* was so named by her Grace in remembrance of her own deliverance from the furye of her enemies, for which she was no lesse myraculously preserved than was the prophet Jonas from the belly of the whale.'

This passage described the first ship to be named after another royal Elizabeth – Queen Elizabeth the First of England (but not of Scotland) – at the time of the Spanish Armada.

And now, four hundred years and many generations of maritime progress later, another similarly named ship was about to face greater perils than ever imagined by the earlier Elizabethan adventurers.

The choice of the Queen's name for No. 552 was challenged however, by the owners of another *Queen Elizabeth* – a 91 gross ton pleasure steamer built in 1924, official number 147670 on the British register, and operated on the Thames by Joseph Mears Launches and Motors of Richmond, Surrey!

In 1940 there would be only two days in the entire year on which a high enough tide would be available giving a sufficient depth of water in the Clyde for the *Queen Elizabeth*'s a safe departure.

The second such occurrence, six months later, could possibly be too late as Glasgow came within the range of enemy bombers. More especially, the *Queen*'s fitting-out berth was required for HMS *Duke of York*. The *Queen* would move out on the first tide of the day and the *Duke* would be moved in on the second.

So shortly after noon on Monday 26th February, after many weeks of correspondence between Cunard and John Brown (much of it secret) – and the subject of much speculation around Clydebank as to the ship's eventual destination – the *Queen Elizabeth* was moved slowly away from her berth, well before the high tide needed to take her downstream.

The order (from the First Lord of the Admiralty, Winston Churchill – concerned at the huge and valuable

For the very first time smoke curls upwards from the *Lizzie*'s forward funnel.
UCS Records/Glasgow University Archives

liner's vulnerability) directing that the vessel should stay away from British waters '... for as long as this order lasts' was about to become a reality.

It took about an hour for the tugs to manoeuvre the liner's head downstream towards the sea and soon word spread amongst the citizens of the town that their ship was off.

Gradually the crowd increased from a few dozen to several hundred as people rushed to vantage points along the Clyde to watch their pride slip quietly – almost furtively – by.

To many her appearance must have come as a bit of a surprise for no longer was she in her pristine Cunard paintwork of black hull and gleaming white superstructure. The one funnel that had been painted red with black bands and a black top had, along with the rest of the ship and the hitherto unpainted funnel, been repainted with a dull uniform Admiralty grey that would give her an anonymity on the broad expanse of the late-winter North Atlantic.

The *Elizabeth* had also been fitted with four miles of rubber coated copper cable, wound around her enormous girth. This coil, suspended almost untidily alongside her fore deck before rising to run beneath the projection of the Promenade Deck, was known as a 'degaussing' coil (named after Dr. Gauss, a nineteenth century expert on magnetism, whose theories had enabled the Germans to produce their new, lethal magnetic mines). Electrically charged it had the effect of neutralising the magnetic field that had been induced in the ship's hull by the constant hammering incurred by the steel structure whilst she was on the slip being built. The object of fitting the coil (one of the first to be so fitted) was hopefully to render the ship immune from the recently introduced menace of the magnetic mine.

Nearly five hours after leaving Clydebank the liner reached the Tail o' the Bank where she anchored.

During her slow and careful trip downriver she had been caught by the flood of the incoming tide and her accompanying tugs had to fight for nearly an hour before the giant could be persuaded not to bury her head into the

Lacking her lifeboats and with a degaussing cable temporarily fixed around her the grey painted mighty *Queen* is eased away from her fitting-out berth.

UCS Records/Glasgow University Archives

bank of the river. Ironically this happened near the spot where the *Queen Mary* had been caught by the wind and, pivoting around, had touched the bank on both sides of the river. She had then earned an entry at Lloyd's as being officially aground, even if for just a few hair-raising minutes.

The next afternoon at a short ceremony held in the Tourist Class Lounge, the *Queen Elizabeth* (official number: 166290) was officially handed over to Cunard – untested and untried. Over the next three and a half days the anchored liner would take on all but eight of her twenty six lifeboats. These had been floated downriver in order to help reduce the liner's weight and thus reduce her draught during that short, critical journey. Even so, the new *Queen* had several thousand tons of weight more than did the *Queen Mary* during that ship's similar journey.

Just over four hundred crew (mostly from the *Aquitania*) joined the *Queen Elizabeth* under the command of Captain Jack Townley, signing articles for a short, coastwise voyage that would ostensibly terminate in Southampton where a hurriedly prepared docking plan – forwarded by the drawing office at John Brown's – had been received by the authorities in the southern port.

Crowds gradually form on the banks of the River Clyde as the *Queen Elizabeth* is carefully escorted from the shipyard to the Tail o' the Bank on Monday 26th February 1940.

Imperial War Museum

A magnificent view of the *Queen Elizabeth* at the start of her flight to safety taken from a British patrol aircraft.

Imperial War Museum

Shipyard workers and officials, using special passes, boarded the ship as she lay at the Tail (if they had not been on board for the short trip) in an attempt to bring some of the hundreds of uncompleted jobs to a satisfactory stage of completion before the ship sailed. The compass was adjusted and many tests were carried out on machinery and other items as the *Queen* waited to sail.

On the 27th, at a boat drill, the assembled crew were told of Churchill's earlier order that the ship was to leave British waters.

This meant that the crew had to sign new foreign articles for an ocean-going voyage. They demanded £50 per man danger money-cum-bonus but were given £30 plus £5 a month extra pay.

Those crew members who, for family or other reasons, declined to sign the new articles were taken off the liner, sworn to secrecy and subsequently spent many hours, practically interned, on board the Southampton tender *Romsey* in a nearby loch.

Not until after the *Elizabeth* had sailed was it considered safe to release them.

The King's Messenger was also constantly awaited as he would bring the order to sail – whether the ship was completed or not. At seven in the morning of Saturday 2nd March the Messenger finally arrived with sealed orders that were only to be opened when the liner was safely out at sea.

The *Queen Elizabeth* weighed her bower anchor half an hour later, at 7.30 am, after putting ashore those remaining shipyard personnel who would not be travelling with the ship.

Joiner Sam Campbell had been put ashore the night before and he recalls that his last sight of the *Lizzie* was from the tug that ferried him to Gourock Pier. As the tug pulled further away the giant liner seemed to disappear into the mist.

Underway at last the *Queen* slipped through the anti-submarine boom that stretched across the Clyde between the Gantocks and the Cloch Lighthouse and headed out to sea. The liner was escorted by aircraft and by four destroyers that would accompany her as far as the Northern Irish coast before she headed into the Atlantic and her

The 'Empress Incognito' arrives in New York on 7th March after her secret Atlantic dash. *Southampton City Museums*

unknown destination, (as yet only still a speculation but in the minds of a well-informed few there were only a few ports in the world that could take a vessel of such a size).

Still having the remains of her launching gear attached to her hull beneath the waterline (this would be removed during the first available dry-docking) it was considered that the liner would be fast enough, if the situation should arise, to outrun any lurking U-boat and avoid any but the most fortunate of well-aimed torpedoes.

Speed would be her best defence in the trying years to come. She was untested, unarmed and – other than for pill boxes and sand bags on the bridge and stern – unprotected.

At eleven o'clock that evening as the liner approached the position where convoys gathered before heading either west or south, Captain Townley opened the sealed orders which had been delivered to the ship shortly before she sailed. After weeks of speculation her destination was at last known: New York! Three hundred and ninety-eight men were scattered around the immensity of the seemingly empty and ghostlike ship, as they settled down to making life on board as pleasant as possible. There were still many unfinished areas in the crew accommodation, some of the men having to make do with bare steel decks. Many electrical cables were unconnected, light fittings still hung unsecured from the deck heads and the lack of heating was keenly felt by those on board.

Carefully edged into her berth by tugs of the Moran fleet, the *Queen Elizabeth* joins her elder sister for the first time and, alongside her, the *Normandie* – still in civilian colours in readiness to hopefully be the "first off the mark" when hostilities finish. Cunard's *Mauretania* is to the right having vacated her berth for the new arrival. *Southampton City Museums*

The three largest liners in the world cast their shadows onto a murky River Hudson. *Normandie* and *Queen Mary* sport funnel covers to protect their propulsion machinery from the elements.   *Southampton City Museums*

Other parts of the ship, however, were finished and in those areas the passengers and crew luxuriated in beautiful carpets and decor. Much of the furniture was covered in dust sheets, giving the interior a feeling of a giant hotel closed down for the winter.

The *Elizabeth*'s call sign was, appropriately enough, GBSS and radio silence was enforced but the wireless room did receive one call at least. This was a signal to alter course in order to avoid a convoy, a precaution against the discovery of the position and course of a *Queen* fleeing into voluntary exile.

Living up to the image of his profession, the purser organised many of the officers and shipyard officials on board into a club called The Unruffled Elizabethans'. With its own printed constitution and with Captain Townley as president, the spirit of the club would seem to remain with the ship throughout the dark years to come: '.... that true Twentieth-Century Elizabethans are able to remain under all conditions completely unruffled'.

During the Atlantic dash members of the club would entertain one another with stories, musical recitals and so on.

One of the members of the 'The Unruffled Elizabethans' was Captain Duncan Cameron. He was the pilot who had taken the *Mary* down the Clyde and was Cunard's choice to do the same for the *Queen Elizabeth*.

After the short trip down the river he had disembarked at the Tail o' the Bank but Cunard insisted that he rejoin the ship for the start of her coastal journey to Southampton: part of the ruse to throw enemy agents off the scent as to her actual destination. Captain Cameron was well and truly

unprepared for the subsequent Atlantic dash, having as his only luggage '... a pocket handkerchief'! However, others on board donated various items of clothing to make up a small and very mixed wardrobe.

There was still plenty of work for the men to do during the few days of the crossing. Tests, inspections and attempting to alleviate a little of the mass of unfinished work that remained in many areas of the ship helped to pass the otherwise uneventful days that blended one into the next.

Some of the men would help the look-outs, constantly on duty, in scanning the sea, sky and horizon for any suspicious movement as the liner sped along between 25 and 27½ knots on a zig-zag course.

At night a strict black-out was observed and to aid this all the windows and portholes had been painted over in the same monotonous grey in which the ship had been coated.

On 7th March, the first sign of outside human existence was observed when a TransWorld Airliner was spotted flying over the ship. This plane carried several reporters and was piloted on this special occasion by the vice-president of the airline company.

The only signs of life on board the ship that the newsmen could see from their vantage point were the figures of just two men waving up at them from the stern of the ship.

Much to the consternation of the crew, New York already seemed to know that the new queen of the ocean, the 'Empress Incognito' as the New York Post called her, was on her way. Listening to a forbidden radio, a crewman had picked up the BBC broadcast which repeated the telling announcement relayed from New York. Suspicions that the *Queen* was on her way must have been strengthened earlier after Cunard's New York office had received orders to move the *Mauretania* from her position on the north side of Pier 90 to another pier further south.

The south side of Pier 90 was occupied by a grey-painted *Queen Mary* and, in the berth next to her, was the French Line's *Normandie*, still resplendent in her peacetime paintwork.

As the *Queen Elizabeth* approached the United States with the steady certainty of 83,000 tons travelling at 30 miles an hour, she steamed by the first ship that had been seen for five days. The sludge-carrier *Coney Island*, outward bound from New York with her loathsome cargo that she was eager to discharge well out to sea, blew three blasts on her single whistle as a courtesy to the grey *Queen* looming ahead of her. As an acknowledgement, the liner replied with a similar signal that boomed forth from her own three deep, richly vibrating sirens.

Five days, nine hours and 3,127 miles after leaving her anchorage in Scotland, the *Queen* passed the Ambrose Channel Light just before 9.30 am, local time.

During that most unusual of maiden voyages her engines had performed beautifully.

After taking on the Sandy Hook Pilot, Captain Townley anchored his ship at Quarantine at 11 am for four hours to await a suitable slack tide that would allow his ship to be safely docked. The stem anchor once again proved its worth.

By now word had spread around the city that the arrival of Britain's newest and mightiest liner was imminent and thousands of people from New York and New Jersey made their way to the vantage points on either side of the River Hudson to watch her come in as planes circled about her and joyous tugs had their high pitched toots regally acknowledged. She docked smoothly and without incident just before 5 pm.

Her Majesty the Queen was delighted to hear of her name-sake's safe arrival and signalled:

'I send you my heartfelt congratulations on the safe arrival in New York of the *Queen Elizabeth*. Ever since I launched her in the fateful days of 1938, I have watched her progress with interest and admiration. Please convey to Captain Townley my compliments on the safe conclusion of her hazardous maiden voyage.

Elizabeth R.'

Churchill was more brief: 'Splendid! Very good indeed. I never had any doubt about her getting over.'

The New York Times succinctly, but admiringly, summarised many pro-British thoughts:

'The world has come to expect naval feats of the British, but there is a quality of sharp surprise and mischievous daring about the *Queen Elizabeth*'s first voyage that electrifies the pulse. The British can take well-justified satisfaction in an opportunity so courageously seized and so adroitly carried out ...'

The article continued, almost lyrically '....Many sagas have begun and ended in our harbour; but can the old-timers remember anything to compare with the unheralded arrival of the biggest and fastest liner in the world, after the most daring of all maiden crossings? It did not matter that the *Queen Elizabeth* wore a drab coat of grey on her first visit to New York or that no brass bands went down the bay to meet her. The interest of New Yorkers was echoed by the admiration of Americans everywhere for those who built her, sailed her and sent her on her way.

'She was due to be launched on that terrible September day in 1938, when the Munich crisis reached its height. The British fleet was mobilised, and peace hung in the balance, too. But no crisis could keep this sea *Queen* from her schedule. For the past six months British shipyards have been crammed with war orders and workers have been pressed relentlessly into war industries; but war was not enough to prevent her or delay her being made ready to sail.

'Neither could the threat of submarines and mines keep her from her first voyage and now she lies safely in a harbour where German bombers cannot harm her.

'Any landlubber can see that the *Queen Elizabeth* is a fine ship, as sleek and graceful as a yacht; a credit to the British merchant marine. Her distinction is not only in being the largest ship in the world; she is also new in design, as the *Queen Mary* was not. The *Queen Mary* was planned before the crossing of the *Bremen*, the *Rex* and the *Normandie*. The *Queen Elizabeth* is the first super-liner to embody the lessons of these maritime pioneers of our streamlined era. The British were right in not leaving such a ship at the mercy of air attack at home. Their luxury liners will have a job to do when the war is over. The dramatic maiden voyage of the *Queen Elizabeth* proves that the British are looking ahead to the days of peace and to the laurels of peace which must be won.'

It was laudable that the New York Times considered that Great Britain and her Allies might be the eventual victors but it was equally strange that they should almost dismiss the super-liners' role as being effective only at the anticipated end of the war.

The arrival of the *Queen Elizabeth* provided those working in and around the city with a unique sight.

For not only had the *Elizabeth*, the grey-painted 'Empress Incognito', joined her elder sister (also painted in similar sombre, but business-like, grey) but the berth next to her intended running companion contained the French Line's chic *Normandie*, the peace-time beauty of the French liner showing slight signs of neglect. She had been laid-up in New York since 20th August the previous year, the gaiety of her lounges silenced, her carpets covered with moth-repellent powder, her furniture draped in sheets.

The world's three largest liners – plus the *Mauretania* – were now together for the first and, as events proved, the last time. Three giants, totalling a quarter of a million tons, dressed in khaki and chiffon but with 'nowhere to go', awaiting the fate imposed upon them by politicians as far dispersed ideologically as they were geographically. By order of the neutral American government (in accordance with the Geneva Convention) only maintenance or construction work of a non-belligerent nature could be carried out on the liners moored along the New York waterfront. The *Queen Mary* had, however, been 'called-up' on 1st March and in the afternoon of 21st March she quietly left her berth: her military career about to begin.

The two sisters would not meet again for another year.

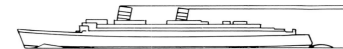

Chapter Six
"The Years of Peril..."
(Churchill)

The *Queen Elizabeth* was now the sole companion of the *Normandie*, a ship to which she owed a debt for her own sleek looks.

The Cunarder was soon transferred to the berth since vacated by the *Queen Mary* and now shared the same rectangle of murky Hudson water as her French counterpart. The latter ship seemed to ignore the young arrival's presence, perhaps secretly resenting the emulation of her own uncluttered upper deck and terraced after decks. She might also have secretly sneered at the *Elizabeth*'s exposed clusters of deck machinery and fittings on the latter's foredeck, a family characteristic that both the *Elizabeth* and her sister shared in common.

The majority of the already reduced crew of the *Queen Elizabeth* left for home on the smaller (20,000 gross tons), twenty year old *Scythia*, also of the Cunard Line. A skeleton crew of just 143 men remained with their charge to maintain her and to oversee the American workmen who now came on board. This labour force came from the nearby Todd Shipyard in Brooklyn and had been contracted to further the completion of the British liner. It was emphasised that no work of a military nature would be undertaken that might affect America's status as a neutral nation.

As a result, the liner found work being carried out on her that would bring her towards completion as the largest merchant ship in the world.

Wooden decks had to be caulked and much of her equipment, which had been brought over as cargo, fitted. Many of the shipboard services such as electric cables still had to be connected, light fittings screwed to deckheads, bare steel castings galvanised, ad infinitum. A lot of her furniture and unnecessary fittings were taken ashore at night to be stored until the day came when they could, hopefully, be reinstated.

The crew, although separated unexpectedly from their families and having had no chance of making their farewells, found – as did their counterparts on the *Mary* – friendship and hospitality from amongst the New Yorkers. However, their shipboard conditions did not compare with those enjoyed by their 'sister-shipmates' who lived on their ship surrounded by her full splendour.

Photographed in New York shortly after her arrival the open upper decks of the liner can be seen to good advantage.
UCS Records/Glasgow University Archives

After leaving her brief lay-up in New York the *Queen Elizabeth* sailed for dry-docking in Singapore. She is seen here at Cape Town *en-route*.   *John Eaton and Charles Haas*

Free passes to theatres, invitations to private homes, the absence of rationing – all contributed towards compensating for being away from home.

Towards the end of the year additional crewmen arrived in New York, having travelled to the city via the British Dominion of Canada. The ship's complement was brought up to four hundred and sixty-five, just sufficient to operate deck, navigating and engineering departments.

The New York newspapers speculated that something was about to happen and, sure enough, on a wet, grey 13th November, at almost 3.30 pm, the *Queen Elizabeth*, heavily laden with fuel and water, quietly slipped out of New York and headed south.

As a final accolade as she pulled away from her berth, a waterside stevedore shouted, almost affectionately: 'Goodbye and good luck, you great big Limey son-of-a-bitch!' His cheer was heard and remembered by Doctor Joseph Maguire who had just joined the liner and who would remain with her throughout the years of her trials – and longer.

Her departure left the *Normandie* alone once again; languishing and, it seemed, left to fend for herself.

The French liner almost seemed abandoned.

But that was not to be. After the Americans were rudely awakened by the unheralded Japanese attack on Pearl Harbour on 7th December 1941 and their consequent entry into the war, the *Normandie* was seized by the U.S. five days later on 12th December.

Work commenced, under the supervision of the Navy, to convert her to a troopship, renaming her U.S.S. *Lafayette*.

Due to the rush, disorganisation and disregard of French routine on board, she caught fire on 9th February 1942, when conversion work was almost complete, capsizing at her berth, top-heavy due to the prodigious amounts of water that had been pumped into her upperworks by the unco-ordinated fire-fighting tugboats.

After providing training for a new generation of naval salvage divers the *Normandie* was later cut-down at the superstructure, righted, towed away and scrapped. An untimely and sordid end to a fine ship whose contribution to the war effort – had things gone right – would surely have equalled the splendid war records of the British *Queens*.

A little while previously, at a meeting held in New York between Cunard and British government officials, it had been decided that the *Queen Elizabeth* should follow in the wake of the *Queen Mary* and become a troop transport. The *Mary* had made her first trooping voyage from Sydney to Scotland on 5th May and, as the *Elizabeth* sailed, rumours as to her destination varied from 'just moving her berth' to 'sailing to Halifax, Nova Scotia.'

But before the second *Queen* could become one of His Majesty's Troop Ships (HMTS) she had to have the remains of the launch gear removed from her bottom plates which would then have to be cleaned and painted. She had been in the water, continuously, for two years.

The liner needed to go into a dry dock somewhere to have this work done and the nearest such facility was in Singapore, then still colonially British. There were only five dry docks in the world that could take liners of the *Queens'* size. The one in Southampton, especially built for the sisters, was unusable because it was within range of Nazi bombers; the use of the American dock at Bayonne was denied because of U.S neutrality; the Esquimalt dock on the west coast of Canada was too far away and the French dock at St. Nazaire (built for the *Normandie*) was out of the question.

To get to Singapore the *Queen Elizabeth* would have to make two stops to take on fuel and water; she had been designed as a five-day voyager.

The liner's first stop would be at Trinidad where she rendezvoused with an oil replenishment tanker five miles off shore to avoid any unwelcome attention.

East transporting urgently needed Australian troops to bolster the defences of Egypt against the enemy's incursions into North Africa.

More than a year after the two *Queens* had last met in New York they sailed in company for the very first time in April 1941. But, as Sydney Harbour was not big enough to allow both ships to anchor at the same time (ie each anchored vessel required a swinging ground of 1,100 feet in radius), one would load her human cargo via tender, usually at night inside the Harbour, whilst the other would lie off in Largs Bay waiting for her partner.

Carrying 5,600 troops on the *Elizabeth* and 6,000 on the *Mary* for the outward trip, the two ships met with other large, but slower, ocean liners to form a spectacular convoy.

Ile de France of the French Line, making a mockery of the 'no-smoking-on-deck-after-dark' routine with a persistent glow emanating from the top of her funnels, Holland America's *Nieuw Amsterdam*, Cunard's own venerable four funneller *Aquitania* (now experiencing duties in a second war) and *Mauretania* plus other famous ships kept the *Queens* company.

Although the *Queens* could easily manage 27-28 knots by themselves, even more when danger was believed to be in the vicinity, they were reduced to the common speed of the convoy of around 20 knots.

Relying on speed and the presence of fast naval cruisers for their defence, the most luxurious liners of peacetime accompanied each other through the Indian Ocean to the Red Sea carrying thousands of troops to stem the eastward ambitions of Nazism and Fascism.

On the return journey the ships carried allied wounded, internees or enemy prisoners-of-war, stopping off at Trincomalee in Ceylon (now Sri Lanka). The Nazi prisoners proved to be particularly arrogant and often gave their despised salute. One Luftwaffe major, who spoke fluent English, decided to boast of his part in the devastating air-raids on Coventry. A young British lieutenant, who had lost his mother and two sisters in these raids, visited this major and subsequently provided Dr. Maguire and his hospital staff with a sudden case of 'unexplained' injuries sustained by the German.

The *Queen Elizabeth* made one welcomed trip to Hobart in Tasmania where their welcome made the ship's complement feel that they were actually appreciated.

Other casualties were caused by the extremely hot weather in which the ships sailed. As the ships were designed for cooler climes there were many cases of deaths caused by heat stroke or by injury caused by frayed tempers in both crew and passengers. Methods were devised to 'cool' such outbreaks, and it also took the *Queens* two and a half days to cool down themselves after arriving at Suez.

Security at sailing and arrival and the safety found in high speed was always paramount and any breach found its lesson learnt in later ventures.

But one particular breach of security that occurred in the Pacific sent shivers down the spines of many. Dr. Maguire wrote of the incident that occurred a day out of Trincomalee.

'..... I awoke suddenly because the engines were slowing down. I slipped into shorts and shirt and went on deck.

Viewed from an escorting cruiser the largest troop transport in the world speeds towards Scotland. *Imperial War Museum*

'My eyes almost refused to believe what they saw.

'The three great ships – the two *Queens* and the *Ile de France* – were stationary. They were huge sitting targets in a hostile ocean. The cruiser (HMAS) *Canberra* had lowered a pinnace which was cruising calmly around collecting bags of mail from each.

'At that moment I remembered that the cruiser, HM(A)S *Sydney* had been sunk by the *Kormoran* without a single survivor a few days before, not so far from our present position. (Her last shells hit the German raider which was abandoned on fire from stem to stern.)

'Now the *Canberra*'s boat crawled around like a sea slug. Time never passed so slowly. At last the pinnace hooked on and a cheery farewell hoist ran up the cruiser's yardarm as she turned for home. I never did find out who was responsible for that risky mid-ocean mail collecting. I know it was the last time the *Queens* ever stopped at sea in war time.'

Between them, in a year spent shuttling between Sydney and Port Tewfik in the Red Sea, the two *Queens* transported nearly 80,000 troops to the war zone.

The *Elizabeth* had quite a lucky escape in August 1941, when steaming through the Red Sea. Enemy spotter planes often flew over the area during the day to provide information of potential targets for their bomber flights which would then arrive at night. On this occasion the *Queen Elizabeth*, completely blacked-out, was steaming astern of the hospital ship *Atlantis* which was brightly lit to identify her as a ship of mercy.

John Havers, a Supply Officer travelling on the *Atlantis*, heard later that an enemy aircraft had flown in low to inspect the hospital ship and in doing so had actually passed between the *Elizabeth*'s funnels!

With Japan and the United States entering the war after the debacle of Pearl Harbour on 7th December 1941, the *Elizabeth* was laid up in Sydney for seven weeks. The Pacific was too dangerous for her with both German and Japanese submarines on the prowl. The Australians also needed what remained of their depleted army for their country's own defence in case of Japanese invasion.

The *Mary* meanwhile had returned to the Clyde but it was decided to send the *Elizabeth* to Canada for dry-docking (that facility in Singapore now being unavailable) as the large amount of tropical growth that fouled the liner's bottom plates needed to be removed. It was estimated that the growth that had attached itself to the hull reduced the ship's speed by a good 2 knots.

Two stops were required for refuelling and watering en route, the first call being made in New Zealand where even the bath tubs of the cautious were filled with fresh water.

The second stop necessitated a call at one of those tiny specks in the vast Pacific, the Marquesas group of islands. A secret rendezvous had been arranged with an American tanker but as the *Elizabeth* steamed into the narrow fjord-like entrance of one of the islands, Nuku Hiva, and sounded her whistle she received no reply. Some natives appeared and promptly disappeared, and a few anxious officers on the Bridge began to wonder where their supplies were. As far as they knew the U-boats that were active in the Pacific could have denied the m the means to continue on the last leg of their journey to Canada.

Ten anxious minutes later the tanker appeared around the headland of the tiny island.

The tension on the liner's Bridge was relieved when one of the officers shouted 'What the hell kept you?' but the tanker's crew were not amused. They had come a long, difficult way; some of their own supplies had run out en route and their flour had gone sour, but their mood eventually mellowed when the larger ship passed over some welcome liquid stores as, being an American ship, the tanker was 'dry'.

Fuelling took eight hours to complete, – an 'orderly rush' – as a report was received that there was a Japanese raider in the area.

Sailing on to Victoria on Vancouver Island, British Columbia, the *Queen* arrived only to miss the tide due to a miscalculation by the ship's officers and had to steam around off the island awaiting the next. When she again came to enter the dry-dock her paravane chains fouled and knocked over some dock-blocks and once more she had to cruise around for twenty-four hours whilst the dock was pumped dry, the blocks reset and the dock re-flooded.

Whilst in Esquimalt dry-dock the ship's bottom was cleaned, the interiors fumigated, guns fitted and the groundwork for the de-gaussing coil that was to be given a permanent, plated-in position (more or less on a level with 'B' deck) was carried out. The final plating-in of the coil would be completed in Scotland.

After Esquimalt the *Queen Elizabeth* sailed for San Francisco and, on arrival, briefly ran aground near the Golden Gate Bridge.

During a conference on board, the U.S. military was told how many men had been transported on the ship on each Sydney-to-Suez trip.

The Americans were characteristically amazed:

'Are you crazy? Only five thousand in THIS monster? We'll fix to send you eight thousand!'

Within five days carpenters had removed the Australian hammocks and bunks and in their place fitted fold-down 'Standee' beds, (made of tubular steel and easy-to-clean canvas webbing) two, three or five to a tier, into every available space. Two days later the *Elizabeth* left in a small convoy bound for Sydney via, once again, the Marquesas with eight thousand American GI's on board needed to bolster Australia's depleted defences until some of their own troops could be recalled from the Middle East.

After disembarking the troops at Sydney, the *Queen Elizabeth* waited for thirteen days until decisions were made as to her future. With a mutually nostalgic farewell the *Queen* sailed out of Sydney on 19th April, with a group of nurses on board destined for Fremantle where they were disembarked.

This was a strange decision as 180 US servicemen, badly wounded in the fighting in the Philippines, had been embarked at Sydney for New York.

German prisoners of war and their Polish guards came on board at Cape Town heading for internment in the USA.

At Rio the ships' searchlights scoured the water around the liner to prevent any escape attempts by the POW's. Armed guards in two motor launches patrolled around the ship but no one had told them that the hospital on board had been allowed to open its portholes whilst in port for ventilation purposes. Subsequently, when one of the patients put his head through the port to get a breath of fresh air, bullets ricocheted from the hull around him!

At last the *Queen Elizabeth* arrived in New York to begin what became known as the 'GI Shuttle', her first such trip departing 5th June.

But another conference took place on board the liner – 'Only eight thousand in a big ship like this? Next trip you sail with ten thousand.'

And so she did. But after the first round voyage the *Queen* would be fitted with a total of twelve thousand Standee bunks (including some along the Promenade Deck) with a special dispensation granted for the gentler Atlantic summer months when an additional three thousand five hundred men could be carried. Many of these men could sleep on the top deck in the open air or else they could 'hot bunk', that is use the Standee bunks on a rotational basis – one soldier using a bunk once it had been vacated by another.

After the *QE*'s arrival in Gourock with her first load of GI's she was then sent to Suez on 17th June, (via Freetown and Simonstown) with reinforcements for the British Eighth Army to help stem Rommel's advances towards the Canal.

The liner returned to New York on 19th August via Capetown, Simonstown and Rio de Janeiro to begin her regular GI shuttle work in earnest. Sometimes she diverted to Halifax, Nova Scotia, to transport Canadian troops to aid in the defence of the Motherland.

In the US the GI's would be gathered at Camp Kilmer in New Jersey for training and instruction on how to board the liners, how to find their cabins, where to stow their kit bags and so on. Giant mockups of the *Queens'* gangway, entrance halls and cabins were built or lined-out for this purpose.

The troops would board which ever of the two ships was berthed at Pier 90 during the late evening hours under cover of darkness after being transported to the Pier by either ferry or bus. The *Queens'* night-time sailings were planned to avoid full moons.

On boarding the *QE* or *Mary* each GI was given a coloured disc or card (red, white or blue) and this indicated the section of ship in which he must remain during the voyage. If he strayed into another section then he was 'fined' by having to assist the crew with their tasks.

Another essential rule was that each man, regardless of rank, should wear or carry his lifebelt when outside his cabin at all times. A transgressor had to forfeit a shoe when caught, having then to hobble back to his cabin to collect the missing belt before being able to retrieve the confiscated footwear.

On leaving New York every soldier had to stand stock still in his allotted cabin until the ship was out to sea. A rush of men to either side to view the famous skyline or the Statue of Liberty would have caused the ship to list. It was calculated that such a list would increase her draught by between two to four feet (with possible damage to both ship and under-river services) and possibly detrimentally affect the ship's stability.

Feeding 10,000 to 16,000 men (depending on the season) twice a day for five days proved to be a mammoth task. A well-narrated shopping list for one trip comprised:

155,000 lb meat and poultry
124,300 lb potatoes
76,000 lb flour and cereal
53,000 lb butter, eggs and milk powder
31,400 lb tea, coffee and sugar and the same amount of canned fruit
29,000 lb fresh fruit
18,000 lb jams
4,600 lb cheese
(2.2046 lb = 1kg)

31,000 eggs at breakfast were boiled in six clean dust-bins into which steam hoses were played for the usual four minutes or so.

US Captain Bill Williams of Kentucky, the messing officer on board *QE* throughout the war, would call the six sittings each of forty-five minutes, 2,000 troops at a time, for the two meals a day (breakfast 6.30 am to 11 am, dinner from 3 pm to 7.30 pm) in his Southern States accent:

'This is the last call for the first sitting in the troops' mess hall. Fahwm yo' lines. This is the last call for chow!' The troops would be then given a pack of sandwiches after breakfast to last them through the day until dinner time.

Although one hundred British and one hundred American full time and voyage-only gunners were carried and regularly exercised, the *Elizabeth* never fired a shot in anger.

Even so, one captain at least would keep the troops below decks during his time in command in 1942 during the voyages from New York to Gourock. Captain Eric Ashton-Irvine (then First Officer) recalled:

'The troops were never permitted on deck during my voyages. Soon after we passed The Narrows in New York harbour, they were sent below and then only to reappear five days later, just after we passed the Clyde lighthouse in Scotland. Only the gunners were permitted on deck. Understandably, should the upper decks be littered with humanity during an attack, the gunners simply could not reach their stations. We would have been lost ...'

During the voyage the troops would keep themselves amused in several ways. The favourites were cards and dice. These games seemed to be never-ending with a man's place in a game quickly being taken should he leave.

On board the *Mary* (and one can assume it was the same on the *QE*) Captain Bisset requested that, as part of keeping the ship clean, the troops should refrain from chewing gum as discarded pieces were difficult to remove from the deck. The practice of carving initials into the ship's teak railings was not discouraged as Captain Bisset resignedly thought: 'Some of them (the troops) would never return, and they knew it. I did not begrudge them the pleasure of carving their initials on the teakwood rails.'

The safety of the troops during these solo, high-speed trooping dashes across the Atlantic was not considered to be paramount in the minds of those at the top. 10,000 men could, perhaps, be carried in safety according to the lifeboat and liferaft capacity of the ship but it was considered that the extra 5,000 men who were carried in summer and not provided for in life saving capabilities was worth the risk, based on the liner's existing records of speed and reliability.

In November 1942, the *QE* was involved in an incident that still remains the subject of much speculation.

The *U-704*, under the command of Kapitan Horst Kessler, was wallowing in a Force 8 gale off the west coast of Ireland heading south returning to base in France.

Early in the afternoon of the 9th a large, two-funnelled steamer was seen through the varying visibility, six to seven miles away.

The submarine dived and the captain identified the ship as the *Queen Elizabeth*. Four torpedoes were fired and the U-boat followed their course. One detonation was heard.

Apparently the torpedo had exploded well away from the ship. The *Queen Mary*'s captain, Bill Bisset, was travelling on the *QE* at the time as a passenger; he said after the war 'There was an explosion near us .... we got up to 31 knots without any trouble!'

Apparently the steamer, observed by Kessler, had been travelling at speed, stopped and, a few minutes afterwards, proceeded on her way.

Kessler has always maintained that the ship was the *Elizabeth* and later, after the war, a Cunard officer told of a detonation near the ship on that same day (all Cunard records from that period have apparently been lost) and

At the end of the war American G.I.s board HMT *Queen Elizabeth* via tender at the Tail o' the Bank for their triumphant return home.

the liner was stopped for fifteen minutes – a forbidden action but obviously considered necessary.

However, to stop the ship would take a considerable time as the superheated steam would need to be cooled to normal working temperatures before slowing the ship could even be considered. This would take an hour at least plus many miles that would not have allowed her to stop within Kessler's observation.

However, rumours had reached New York that the *Queen Elizabeth* had been sunk with the likelihood that she had taken many men down with her.

Staff Captain Harry Grattidge of the *Queen Mary* had heard the unconfirmed reports whilst presiding over lunch-time drinks in his cabin as the liner lay alongside her berth in New York.

The resulting gloomy lunch-hour was just coming to an end when the telephone rang. It was the girl at the Cunard Exchange on the Pier Head.

Harry Grattidge wrote of the conversation in his autobiography, 'Captain of the *Queens*':

' "Captain," she gulped, "Oh, Captain – the *Queen Elizabeth*.."

' "I know," I said patiently. "It's terrible news."

'She almost squawked in her excitement. "No, no, you don't understand. Oh Captain, it was all a rumour ... She's here. She's just anchored at Quarantine ...."

' "Gentlemen," I said, replacing the receiver, "will anyone refuse a glass of wine when I tell then that the *Queen Elizabeth* is with us now, safe and sound?"

'There was not a dissenting voice. We charged our glasses. It was Henry Morganthau who raised his first: "To the two great ladies of the Atlantic – the *Queens*' "

Five weeks before this incident the *Queen Mary* had been involved in a more tangible, more substantial accident. On 2nd October, the three-funnelled liner was approaching the north coast of Ireland en route to Gourock from New York with thousands of GI's on board.

The Royal Naval cruiser HMS *Curacoa* had come out to meet and escort the liner into home waters and, as usual, set off in the direction of England at high speed as soon as the smoke from the *Mary*'s funnels was sighted over the horizon.

The Cunarder soon caught up, both ships maintaining their synchronised zig-zag.

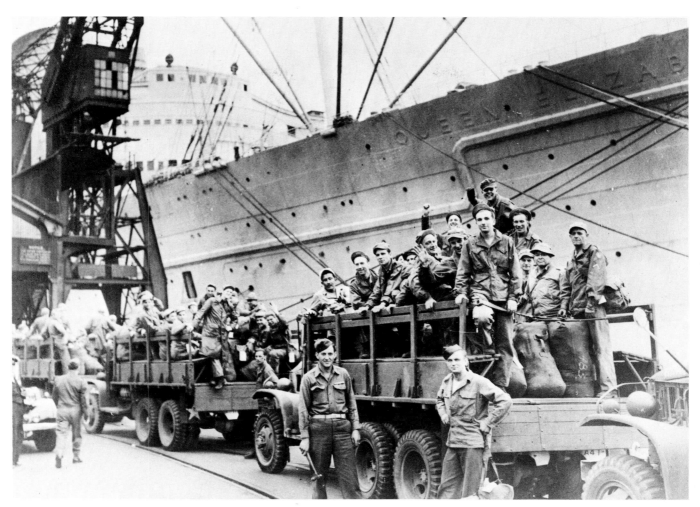

After the *Queen*'s first visit to Southampton in August 1945, the repatriation of G.I.s took place directly from the dockside.

Imperial War Museum

The cruiser's zig-zag gradually went out of phase with that of the liner and soon the upset pattern decreed that the naval ship should cross the path of the oncoming troopship.

Unhappily, fortune took a sad turn and the *Queen Mary*'s bow sliced through the cruiser's hull like a knife through butter.

The liner, with buckled stem and flooded fore-peak, had to carry on at reduced speed whilst four other destroyer escorts remained behind to pick up survivors from the two quickly-sunk sections of the cruiser. Out of four hundred and ten sailors on board HMS *Curacoa* only seventy-two survived.

The comfort and well-being of the men on the *Queens* was considered as far as it was possible to do so – but the North Atlantic itself was still a force to be reckoned with.

On one particular crossing from Gourock to New York the *Lizzie* ran into a very heavy storm when two days out into the Atlantic.

Fortunately, being on a westbound trip, the liner was not full carrying, amongst others, British service personnel to various postings in the United States. Some passengers helped to pass their days by helping the crew with anti-submarine lookout duties.

Charles Harrison, on his way to a naval posting, remembered that amongst the civilian passengers on board was Irving Berlin who played the piano and sang some of his own songs.

The storm was particularly violent and the *Queen* hove-to for about two days, making under 10 knots. Doctor Maguire recounted what happened in his autobiography 'The Sea my Surgery':

'We were driving far to the north, risking heavy weather we would normally have dodged on a peace-time run. Head-seas smashed heavily against our 83,000 tons of ship.

'My wrist-watch showed eight o'clock in the morning and I was thinking of getting up. My mind was suddenly made up for me.

'We suddenly hit a freak sea, a great mountainous mass of green water. The *Queen Elizabeth*'s bows rose skyward and then disappeared down into a vast trough. As she did so another enormous roller came from nowhere and punched her bows even further downwards. We just continued to go down. I was thrown clean out of bed and could not stand upright.

'This is it', I thought, even though I couldn't believe it. There was a deafening roar like nothing I have ever heard before. Every plate vibrated as our propellers rose up out

41

of the sea and raced in thin air. For a measureless moment the ship seemed to stand up on her nose. Finally, slowly, so very slowly, she dragged her fore-part from the water, and I found I had been holding my breath.

'Then the loud-hailers started booming, calling for carpenters and joiners from the troops we were carrying to New York. Every skilled man was needed – fast.

'That colossal sea had punched the ship's fore-deck down and out of shape by six inches. The fore-peak was flooded. Every forward capstan was out of commission. Both anchors were jammed.'

As will be remembered, the *Queen Mary* had a forward well-deck in which green seas could spend their force before breaking against the bridge. As this eventuality had never arisen the well-deck had been omitted on the *Queen Elizabeth*, an omission that was now to be regretted. Doctor Maguire continued:

Eager to get home, American soldiers clamber on board at Southampton. *Imperial War Museum*

'The second vicious sea had also smashed squarely against the bridge, shattered the thick plate-glass windows, washed the quartermaster from the wheel-house to the wing of the bridge.

'The Staff Captain, whose cabin was immediately under the bridge, had been shaving when it struck. A block of plate glass from his window was stove in, in one piece, ricocheted from a panel, hit him flat, and knocked him down. In two seconds he was sitting, dazed, waist-deep in water.

'When I went up to attend to him I talked to a white-faced officer on the bridge. He was suffering from minor shock. His line of vision, he told me, as the *Elizabeth* went down and down towards the bed of the ocean was from the bridge window, through to the crow's nest on the fore-mast to where the ship's bows should normally have been. The hawse-pipes, like huge frightened eyes, must have been staring straight down towards the bottom of the Atlantic.

'And from that frightening episode, I had two minor casualties!'

From the officer's description of looking through the crow's nest from his position on the bridge, the liner must have been heading to possible destruction at an angle of around 60°

Some men weren't so lucky on another rough crossing the previous Christmas. Dennis Money had boarded at Gourock and recalled that only five hundred of those passengers on board attended Christmas lunch.

'One of the most bizarre experiences still vivid in my mind was attending the Christmas Eve carol service in what was the first class lounge – lush even in wartime garb. Those attending were seated in wicker armchairs, the splayed feet of which sank into deep-piled carpet. Midway through the service, the ship suddenly heeled over in excess of 30° and like some fantasy, all the passengers slid towards the bulkhead. Needless to say, the programme continued. Afterwards, we learnt that the sonar had picked up a submarine sounding and the helm of the *Queen Elizabeth* was flung over – the ship making a 45° change in direction.

'The culmination of events occurred when the *Queen Elizabeth* was caught between the crests of some 40 ft waves during the night and dropped bodily into the trough, resulting in many injuries, including three fatalities, when those manning the guns on the upper decks plunged to their deaths as the ship plummeted down. Among the most seriously injured were those accommodated in the troop quarters aft in five-tiered bunks. When the ship literally dropped, many of those in the upper bunks crashed down on the deck below. Fortunately, I was housed in one of the adapted first-class cabins and landed with a jolt safely on my bunk. The severity of the accident was clearly visible the next morning. The huge steel stanchions to the foremast had been torn away together with all the 'Carley floats' attached to them.'

After this horror it was a special pleasure to arrive safely in port, especially one like New York. Denis Money recalls:

'After the months of black-out experienced in and around the UK it was like a fairyland to sail into the tranquil waters past the Statue of Liberty and to see the twinkling lights of the renowned New York skyline.'

The sheer pleasure of arriving in a lightened, bustling, bomb-free city on board the world's largest ship after a pleasant Spring crossing is also remembered by Denis Morrell of Barking:

'At the age of 67 (in 1987) I can look back with great pleasure and affection at my one and only encounter with *Queen Elizabeth*.

'At the age of 20 I had departed from Nottingham for the Royal Navy, a snotty-nosed kid whose main thrill in life had come from sundry day trips to Skegness.

'I had completed my telegraphist training at HMS *Royal Arthur* (ie Butlins Holiday Camp, Skegness – "Our True Intent Is All For Your Delight"), spent eighteen months on a Submarine Depot Ship, resting on a pile of empty corned beef tins in the Firth of Clyde, and had successfully swapped a draft to HMS *Flamingo* (ie Bombay) for a mysterious assignment called, I think, JX232.

'We left Chatham Barracks in April 1943, on this unknown venture. We found ourselves heading for Glasgow. Before much time had elapsed we were on a small boat heading for a grey hulk in the middle of the Clyde. The small, grey ship soon became enormous.

'It was indeed the *Queen Elizabeth*, newly fitted out and given the job of transporting the Army, Navy and Air Force between the Old and New Worlds. It (the ship) went so fast that there was very little likelihood of a U-boat confrontation.

'What a wonderful ...crossing that was! We were given the job of washing up after hoards of airmen had gorged themselves on the magnificent food which was available. We were quartered down below in the bows where bunks rose and fell six feet as the giant sped along. Although it was April, and the North Atlantic, I do not remember ever feeling cold.

'There was a joyous atmosphere everywhere on board. Could it be that we were all delighted to get away from war-torn Europe, at least for a little while? At night the upper decks were filled with music from guitars or mouth-organs. The snotty-nosed provincial kid was overwhelmed with happiness.

'And then came the early morning sight of New York. As a child I had time after time considered that if ever I got to Heaven it would be going round Woolworth's in New York, and there it was, perhaps the most dramatic vista in all the world's history.

'We cruised up the Hudson River to Pier 90, passing the terrible sight of the *Normandie*, burnt out and on its side near one of the piers. We left the *Queen Elizabeth* and I never saw her again until the newsreel shots of her ... in Hong Kong harbour.

'But it was the *Queen Elizabeth* that took me to a magic world of Frank Sinatra singing "I Couldn't Sleep a Wink Last Night", to Harry James, to Fred Waring and his Pennsylvanians, to Boris Karloff acting in "Arsenic and Old Lace", to the top of the Empire State Building. It was the *Queen Elizabeth* that introduced me to the overwhelming generosity and kindness of the American people.

'Later there was Asbury Park, and meeting two Dorothy's either of whom I could have married; there was Montreal and the River-class frigate *Barle*. There was Jeanette Macdonald in an important operatic debut in Montreal. There was St. John's and Halifax, the return to Europe, Gibraltar, a new ship – the destroyer *Kempenfelt*, and Scapa Flow.

'Later still there was Naples, and the Suez Canal, and Anzio and D-Day. There was demob and marriage and children and the Civil Service and several houses. After *Queen Elizabeth* there were 44 years of the ups and downs of life. But the memory of that Atlantic crossing in that great ship burns brightly always in my memory.'

Other passengers were less enthusiastic at seeing the 'twinkling lights of the New York skyline' for the first time. These were the German POW's travelling, 4,000 at a time on both *Queens*, to internment in the United States. They had been informed, through Nazi propaganda, that a blacked-out New York skyline was in bombed ruins. What a surprise they had!

Altogether the *Queen Elizabeth* made thirty-five crossings of the Atlantic during which time, and for a while after, she was under American control through a lease-lend arrangement. She had, however, remained all the while under Cunard management with British officers and crew.

Throughout the years of the 'GI shuttle' the two *Queens* had never been in the same port at the same time and avoided full-moons whilst at Gourock. They had quietly left New York, steaming by the sad hulk of the *Normandie* gradually decaying through the final act of salvage, impressing many New Yorkers as they efficiently went about their business.

Heading for Gourock and their safe anchorage amongst the magnificent hills of the Scottish countryside they would disgorge their whole battalions of GI's into paddle steamers and other tenders for onward transmission to camps dispersed throughout the British Isles. Here the GI's would wait and train before taking part in the enormous achievement of D-Day – the Invasion of Europe – and the ultimate defeat of Hitler and his insidious reign of terror.

After being cleaned by a small army of cleaning ladies and being replenished with fuel and stores, the *Queens* would then take on a lesser number of returning wounded, POW's and British civil and military passengers heading for the USA, Canada and other destinations.

By the end of May 1945 the *Queens* had carried between them, in both directions, a staggering 1,243,538 passengers. On the North Atlantic alone totals of 869,694 people had been carried eastwards and 213,008 transported between Gourock and New York. The *QE* had, between April 1941 and March 1945 steamed 492,635 miles and carried 811,324 'souls'. The highest number she had carried at any one time was 15,932 passengers and crew but the record for the highest number ever carried in one ship went to the *Mary* with 16,683!

Many famous people travelled to and fro on the *Queens* during the period of the war en route to political or theatrical engagements. Winston Churchill, unable to travel by 'plane due to a tubercular complaint, travelled on the *Mary* to meetings in the US and Canada on three occasions. Perhaps the most famous visitor to the *Elizabeth* was the self-exiled ex-king Edward VIII (Duke of Windsor); he visited the liner in New York between trooping voyages.

The *Queen Elizabeth* happened to be in New York both on VE Day when her whistle joined that of the *Mary* in the noisy celebrations of the joyous occasion. She was also there on VJ Day three months later.

It now fell to the *Queens* to transport back to their homelands many of the hundreds of thousands of GI's they had brought to Europe and, in the *Mary*'s case, transport some 25,000 American servicemen's 'War Brides' and their children to their new home country.

And so, on 24th June 1945, the *QE* left Gourock with her first load of returning GI's. Their welcome in New York was, to say the least, tumultuous with a 'blimp', bands on small ships and a ticker-tape shower cascading from the waterfront buildings welcoming 'the boys' home.

The *Elizabeth* left Gourock for the last time as a troopship on 7th August, bringing to an end a long and close association that had been surrounded by maximum security, because of its vital importance. As she left she signalled, simply but sincerely, 'Thank you, Gourock'.

The next time the *Queen Elizabeth* would berth in the United Kingdom it would be in Southampton, the port which should have received her six years previously.

At last, she was coming home.

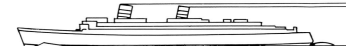

Chapter Seven

".... the World's Fresh Ornament"
(Sonnet I)

In a dull, steady drizzle the still grey-painted *Queen Elizabeth* carefully steamed past the Nab light tower into the eastern approaches of Spithead.

Soon the three, dome-like, stone structures of Palmerston's forts – his 'follies' – passed the ship astern off Bembridge. She sailed on into the Solent and towards Cowes where she turned to starboard to glide between the Brambles and Shingles sandbanks that guarded the entrance to Southampton Water.

Another turn, this time to port, brought the ship's bow around Calshot Spit, before she headed up the water towards Southampton Docks.

The Red Funnel tug which had met the huge liner off Ryde remained with her just in case her services were needed.

The day, Monday 20th August 1945, was an auspicious – if underplayed – day. Four and a half years late,

the liner was making her first visit to the port which had been deceived into believing that the *Lizzie* was on her way there back in February 1941. For its enthusiasm the port had, instead, received a visit from an equally deceived Luftwaffe.

Now all was forgiven. 'Southampton's Baby' – as the Cunarder was described later in the day by the city's mayor – was at last coming home.

But the reception that bomb-torn Southampton proffered differed greatly from that given to the ship when she arrived in New York carrying the first batch of fifteen thousand returning heroes.

With other ships in the port sounding the three dots and a dash of the 'Victory-V' morse sign on their sirens the *Queen Elizabeth* slid into her berth on the River Test just before midday.

The *Queen Elizabeth*'s first departure from Southampton in August 1945 was marked by a fly past of eight Meteor jets; almost 16,000 returning G.I.s were on board the liner.

Imperial War Museum

The fourteen-piece Southampton Borough Police Band played on the quayside. Cunard's house flag, flanked on either side by the flags of Great Britain and the United States, hung rain-sodden and limp from the adjacent passenger shed.

The small crowd of spectators fell silent as the tugs gently brought the great, grey, cliff-sided vessel alongside the quay.

As the British and American national anthems came to an end the band packed up and hurried off. And that was that! The Mayor of Southampton and other civic dignitaries boarded the vessel and made speeches of welcome. Captain E.M. Fall, who had succeeded Captain Townley and had commanded the *QE* throughout much of the war, replied on behalf of the ship.

Three days later the Commodore of the Cunard–White Star Line – and recently ennobled – Sir James Bisset ('Bill' to his friends) took over the command of the *Queen Elizabeth* on Captain Fall's retirement.

Commodore Bisset had previously been in command of the *Queen Mary*, joining that ship in 1942 and sailing with her throughout much of the 'GI Shuttle'. During this period he had taken over command of the *Elizabeth* for two voyages in 1942. It was during his absence that the *Mary*, under Captain Illingworth, had cut her escorting cruiser – HMS *Curacoa* – in half. Trained in sail, as most Cunard skippers then were, Bill Bisset had many years earlier been Fourth Officer on the *Carpathia*, the ship that had responded to a famous distress call in April 1912, subsequently rescuing survivors of the great White Star liner *Titanic* which had struck an iceberg and foundered on her maiden voyage with great loss of life.

Happily, the *Queen*'s first departure from Southampton was more of a celebration in the grand style. Full of GI's happy to be returning home the liner was given a send-off to match the occasion. Eight 'Meteor' jets provided an exciting military salute, flying in formation over the liner as she pulled away from her berth.

The 14,996 passengers – which included thirty civilians amongst the war's bravest GI's (a bravery that had earned them the right to be the first to be repatriated) – was USAF Colonel James Stewart – famed film star in the days of peace but an 'All American' airforce hero during the war. Amongst the embarked civilian passengers was the *Queen Elizabeth*'s first actual fare-paying passenger, Mr Sam Berlin.

The *QE* would make three voyages from Southampton repatriating US servicemen until Britain requested her return to British control to repatriate British and Dominion personnel. The *Queen Mary* would continue under American guidance for a while longer carrying thousands of 'GI Brides' to their new homes in the States.

During the *Elizabeth*'s turn around in New York on her second GI trip from Southampton, Commodore Bisset had the liner's grey funnels repainted in Cunard's red and black on 24th September. The result brightened up the ship considerably '... after the years of drabness' and seemed to reflect the anticipated joys of the peaceful years to come.

On the *QE*'s last such trip she carried what was believed to be her greatest number ever – 15,077 GI's and other passengers and 855 crew – a total of 15,932.

From 22nd October, the *Queen*'s job would be to repatriate thousands of Canadian soldiers home from defending the Motherland.

It was considered appropriate that a British ship should be used for repatriating British citizens, Canadians outwards and British Far East Prisoners of War home eastwards (the latter men travelling across Canada from Vancouver where they had arrived from the Far East). It was, however, also considered unpractical for the *Queen* to venture further abroad to other ports in other countries which might either not be able to accommodate the liner or the ports themselves might be in states of disrepair or mined. The reduced numbers likely to be carried on longer voyages also tipped the balance in favour of purely North Atlantic voyages.

The Canadian Government had hoped that the *Queen Elizabeth* would be able to disembark their soldiers at Halifax, Nova Scotia. And so it was to this port, easy of access and on a shorter route than New York, that the *Queen* triumphantly arrived on 26th October with 12,517 jubilant passengers and 864 crew, four days after leaving Southampton where the soldiers had showered cigarettes and coins on to the crowd of spectators.

However, Commodore Bisset, although delighted with the reception given to his ship, was not happy with the location of the quay alongside which the *QE* was berthed. He considered the site too exposed should a strong south-easterly wind spring up; this would cause his ship to range back and forth, possibly breaking her moorings, causing damage to both ship and quay.

In spite of understandable Canadian protestations that they wanted their soldiers to step directly onto Canadian soil, Bill Bisset recommended that future repatriations should be either to New York or to Boston from where the Canadian citizens could be transported back to Canada by rail. The Commodore considered the safety of his ship to be paramount and he would not be persuaded otherwise.

On the return from the first trip to Halifax the *Queen* carried the Canadian Prime Minister, the Honourable Vincent Massey, his wife and state officials. Amongst the other passengers were many British POW's returning from internment in the Far East.

Typical of these was A.C. Humphries of Sholing, Southampton.

He remembered the *Lizzie* with affection, writing to the Southampton Echo at the end of her career:

'It is October 1946 in Halifax, Nova Scotia. 1200 men are returning home from a living Hell, from 3½ years of captivity under the Japanese. We helped build the 'Railway of Death'; had been shipped to Japan; had smelted zinc; mined coal; laboured on the Docks. Had been beaten, starved and humiliated. Now we were coming home, on the finest ship the World had ever seen, a British ship, and we were proud to be British.

'As this Giant of the Seas eased slowly away from the quayside, we were finally on the last lap of our long journey home.

'We have not been accustomed to such luxury, quite a change from prison camps.

'Commodore Sir James Bisset is in command and the Right Hon. Vincent Massey, Mr Philip Noel Baker,

Flag bedecked, the *Queen Elizabeth* arrives in New York for the first time with thousands of returning G.I.s on board.
Author's collection

In October the *Queen*, with funnels repainted in Cunard colours, delivered a shipload of Canadian soldiers back to their homeland. In spite of the welcome her skipper was not happy with the exposed berth at Halifax, Nova Scotia.
Author's collection

General Sir Hastings Ismay and 'Wee' Georgie Wood are sailing with us.

'English food, English beer, English cigarettes, the first for four years – we were in clover. November in the North Atlantic didn't worry us, we were coming home.

'Four days went by quickly, but not quickly enough. 'Wee' Georgie organised and compered a concert, and the captain and the VIPs addressed the audience with words of welcome and encouragement. Nearly everyone attended a church service, voluntarily, to give thanks for our deliverance.

'Monday November 5th is 'The Day'. Everyone is up on deck bright and early to catch a first glimpse of England, to be met by a thick November fog. As she slowly edged her way up Southampton Water, her deep siren blaring out its warning I was constantly being asked "Where are we now?" or "How much farther?", but I couldn't see through the fog to tell them.

'The Dock Head came into view, then the turn to starboard, tugs manoeuvred her into the berth, a military band played us in. A "Welcome Home" speech by the Mayor of Southampton was followed by one from Southampton's new M.P. Dr. Horace King.

'Many of the men unashamedly allowed a tear to trickle down their cheeks as the full realisation came that we were really home and remembered those that we had left behind, never to return.

'Of all the hundreds of thousands of miles she sailed in her long career, that was probably classed as just another uneventful trip, but to that small band of men, of whom I was privileged to be one, it was the 'Journey of a Lifetime'. For me the *Queen Elizabeth* will always be "The Ship That Brought Me Home!" '

On arrival in Southampton the *Queen* was dry-docked, using for the very first time the King George V dock which had been specially built for her sister and herself more than ten years previously.

The *QE*'s first Christmas of peacetime was spent at sea, en voyage for New York. The trip was unfortunately rough and not all the 13,272 Christmas dinners that had been prepared were eaten!

Quite often on the return journey from New York the *Elizabeth* would carry fewer than a thousand passengers.

The liner's first departure from Southampton in the New Year of 1946 found a special VIP amongst her 12,314 passengers. After successfully directing Britain's war as Prime Minister against the now crumbled malignant influence of Nazism, Winston Churchill found himself voted out of office and en route for a three month holiday in Florida.

Boarding the ship dressed in his Trinity House uniform of yachting cap and brass-buttoned coat and clutching an inevitable cigar, he and his wife posed for the cameras at the top of the gangway.

It would be Churchill's first voyage in the *Queen Elizabeth*, although he had travelled on the *Mary* on several occasions during the war heading westwards for top-level conferences in Canada and the United States.

Now, on the day before berthing in New York, he broadcast a special, but typical of his style of oration, speech to the troops on board although it went unreported by the press: 'My friends and shipmates in the *Queen Elizabeth*!

'For most of you it is homeward-bound. It has been a good voyage in a great ship, with a fine Captain – or indeed Commodore. We have not got there yet, but I am quite sure he will find the way all right. At any rate, he has been over the track before, and, as I can testify myself, having been several times with him, in those days there used to be U-boats and things like that. They all seem to have dropped off now and we don't have to worry about them at all. Something has happened. The seas are clear, the old flag flies, and those who have done the work, or some of it – because the British did some – turn home again, their task accomplished and their duty done.

'What a strange fearful, yet glittering chapter this war has been! What changes it has brought throughout the world and in the fortunes of so many families! What an interruption in all the plans each of us had made! What a surrender of the liberties we prized! What a casting away of comfort and safety! What a pride in peril! What a glory shines on the brave and true! The good cause has not been overthrown. Tyrants have been hurled from their place of power, and those who sought to enslave the future of man-kind have paid, or will pay, the final penalty.

'You Canadians, many of whom served in the Canadian Fifth Division, no doubt have your minds filled with the victorious war scenes of Italy and the Rhine. But we Englishmen always think of the days of 1940, when the Canadian Army Corps stood almost alone in Kent and Sussex, and the Germans had twenty-five divisions ready to leap across the Channel and wipe Great Britain out of life and history. I think about those days, too, sometimes, and how fine it was to see everyone, at home and throughout the Empire, moved by the same impulse, so simple, so sublime – "Conquer or die!"

'Victory in arms, or in any walk of life, is only the opportunity of doing better on a larger scale and at a higher level. Do not be anxious about the future! Be vigilant, be strong, be clear-sighted, but do not be worried. Our future is in our hands. Our lives are what we choose to make them. The great British Commonwealth and Empire, emerging from the fire once again, glorious and free, will form a structure and an organisation within which there will be room for all, and a fair chance for all.

'Yesterday I was on the bridge, watching the mountainous waves, and this ship – which is no pup – cutting through them and mocking their anger. I asked myself, why is it that the ship beats the waves, when they are so many and the ship is one? The reason is that the ship has a purpose, and the waves have none. They just flop around, innumerable, tireless, but ineffective. The ship with the purpose takes us where we want to go.

'Let us therefore have purpose, both in our National and Imperial policy, and in our own private lives. Thus the future will be fruitful for each and for all, and the reward of the warriors will not be unworthy of the deeds they have done.'

Churchill's words had provided meaningful inspiration and hope during the war years for countless millions. Now, in what was perhaps the last of many such fine orations,

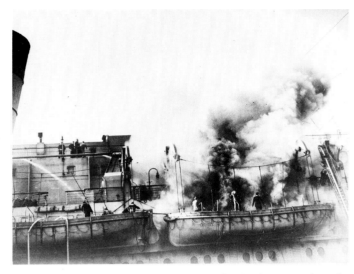

Two days before her demobilisation a fire broke out on board the liner. Firefighters and their equipment were lifted to Boat Deck level using the ship's boats as lifts.

Imperial War Museum

he was quietly exiting the world's stage, leaving behind his final encouraging words of peace.

During the recent conflict the *Queen Elizabeth* had carried much valuable cargo (other than for 750,000 troops, as Commodore Bisset was proud of relating). After safely delivering Winston Churchill to American shores the liner returned to Southampton carrying one of the most priceless pieces of cargo that she had ever carried – the Lincoln Cathedral copy of the Magna Carta.

Stored in a copper lined metal case it was due to be stored in a safety deposit box placed within the liner's strong room. Unfortunately the deposit box was just half-an-inch too large to fit into the assigned strong room safe so Commodore Bisset decided on another place of safe storage-in his own cabin under his bed!

The *Lizzie* made two further trips to New York repatriating Canadian troops.

On 6th March, when the liner arrived back in Southampton, the Ministry of War Transport announced that the *Queen Elizabeth* would be the first ocean going passenger ship to be released from His Majesty's Government service. She was to become to a post-war Britain what the *Mary* had represented to the country after the Great Depression – a national symbol of recovery from adversity.

For the *Lizzie* the war was over. Together, the *Queens'* war records stood second to none. Sir Percy Bates said that he liked to think that the *Queens* had, by their troop carrying capacities, shortened the war by a whole year. Churchill agreed, succinctly summing up the Cunard liners' important contribution:

'Built for the arts of peace and to link the Old World with the New, the *Queens* challenged the fury of Hitlerism in the Battle of the Atlantic. At a speed never before realised in war, they carried over a million men to defend the liberties of civilisation.

'Often whole divisions at a time were moved by each ship. Vital decisions depended upon their ability continuously to elude the enemy, and without their aid the day of final victory must unquestionably have been postponed. To the men who contributed to the success of our operations in the years of peril, and to those who brought these two

The *Queen Elizabeth* was transformed from a drab troopship into the world's most luxurious liner whilst laying at anchor at the Tail o' the Bank. Thousands of men and tons of equipment were ferried out to her. The Royal Navy's newest battleship, HMS *Vanguard*, is seen passing the moored liner *en-route* from completion at John Brown's shipyard to her own trials.

George Outram & Co Ltd, Glasgow

great ships into existence, the world owes a debt that it will not be easy to measure.'

So much for the cynics who, in the early days of the war, prophesied that the *Queens* would lie uselessly alongside their safe pier in New York for the duration of the war!

As a preliminary to the normality of peace that the *Queen Elizabeth* had not yet known, two hundred and fifty tons of fittings – including 10,000 standee bunks and 12,000 lifejackets – had already been taken off the ship in New York. Now, back in Britain, the major job of converting the liner into a passenger ship – including completing work that had been left unfinished by John Brown's in 1941 – was to be undertaken.

During the months preceding the end of the war Cunard and the shipyard had been corresponding, discussing the anticipated conversion. Timetables drawn up by Cunard were considered to be arbitrary by John Brown's as it had been tentatively agreed that the *Queen Elizabeth* should spend twelve weeks on the Clyde (at her old wartime anchorage off Gourock as she could not now reach the ship-yard) plus ten weeks alongside Berth 101 in Southampton's Western or 'New' Docks and in the King George V dry dock.

Half the ship's crew was paid-off and went on leave whilst around four hundred remained with the ship for maintenance, fire watch and to sail the ship on the coastwise journey to the Clyde.

But before any of the complex plans for conversion could be realised the *Queen*'s future was almost denied to her only two days before her release from active service.

The *Queen Elizabeth* had just come through five years of warfare and its aftermath relatively unscathed other than for the wear and tear of the active service on which she had been employed.

True, some minor attempts of sabotage had been made. Bombs had been found on board in New York in the early days of the war (these had been thrown overboard before it could be determined whether they were dummies or 'for real'); bottle caps had reportedly been found blocking hoses and holes had been drilled into some lifeboats. The *Queen*, however, escaped the sad fates of the *Normandie* and *Empress of Britain* and many other fine liners lost either through enemy action or accident.

But at 8.50 on the morning of Friday 8th March 1946, two waiters, Barlow and Cartright, saw smoke pouring from the one-time Isolation Hospital on the Promenade Deck. The hospital had not been used as such for some time and had recently been used as a medical store room containing, amongst other things, bottles of ether, methylated spirit and other inflammable substances. The room was also, apparently, the only room on the ship not to have been fitted with automatic sprinklers!

Fire bells alerted the Commodore and crew and, before fans could be shut off, smoke crept into the ventilation trunking, finding its way into other areas of the ship.

Fire doors were shut and the crew attempted to fight the fire with hoses connected to deck hydrants. But the smoke was too dense to get near the seat of the fire and the firefighters were few – many of the trained men having gone home on leave.

Within minutes, it seemed, fire appliances from Southampton's Fire Brigade arrived on the dockside; other units were called from surrounding towns in Hampshire and Wiltshire. Bournemouth, Salisbury, Winchester, Eastleigh, Totton, Lyndhurst, New Milton and Hythe sent engines to help fight what could easily become a major disaster. Fire floats from Southampton and the Isle of Wight were also alerted.

Other large liners were in the berths adjacent to the *Elizabeth* – the *Mary* and *Aquitania* were due in over the next few days – and, as sabotage was the initial summation, guards were brought into the docks.

As the dense smoke continued to billow into the sky from the threatened liner the shore firemen tried to reach the seat of the fire by using their telescopic ladders. Unfortunately the ladders could not reach high enough for the firemen to direct the water jets efficiently onto the seat of the fire. Luckily Commodore Sir James Bisset was a resourceful man and he ordered that the lifeboats in the vicinity of the fire be lowered; he then had the firemen, with their immediate equipment, clamber into them. The lifeboats were then hoisted to Promenade Deck level from where the firemen could easily tackle the fire from an effective point of attack.

Water was also played into the cabins and public rooms bordering the seat of fire in order to cool them. It took three hours to extinguish the blaze.

Damage sustained by the liner consisted of several heavy steel beams (supporting the Boat Deck) warping and bulging the deck above into a huge blister. Damage to other parts of the liner had been caused by smoke and water and the final cost of damage was £14,000 (in 1946 terms).

'Sabotage' was the favourite word of the day but, after studying photographs of the damage and the available evidence, Dr R. B. Firth (the UK's foremost fire expert who had been called in to investigate the fire) thought otherwise. He concluded that it had 'probably' been caused by a workman who had gone into the Isolation Hospital for a quiet smoke not noticing – or ignoring – the fumes emanating from a broken bottle of medical spirit!

The *Elizabeth* lay at Southampton with her small caretaker crew and three hundred men from John Brown's (there was a drastic shortage of local skilled men) on board taking off as much of the ship's wartime fittings – such as temporary toilets, wash stands, associated piping, etc. – prior to the ship sailing north for her major reconditioning.

On 30th March, she sailed, arriving and anchoring at Gourock the next day.

It was out of the question for the *Queen* to sail up the Clyde to the shipyard so it was planned that men and equipment would be ferried out to the liner as she lay anchored at the Tail.

The shipyard manager, William MacFarlane, would have preferred the *Queen* to have anchored alongside the jetty at Gareloch where direct rail access was available, but Cunard objected to the plan as, like Halifax, it would expose the liner to danger if a strong wind blew from a particular quarter.

Cunard's engineering department was concerned at the length of time that the *QE* would be anchored at the

Tail o' the Bank as the liner would need to have the engines, that were not under survey, running. This would enable the liner to be manoeuvred if necessary but it would also mean continuous operation that might place too great a strain on the machinery.

Cunard had allowed the shipyard just ten weeks to complete the mammoth task of restoring and completing the ship's structure – the largest ever such task to be completed afloat. In spite of the shipyard's protestations and pleas for more time it was done.

According to one estimate the liner had experienced the equivalent of 25 years of normal wear in five years because she had not had the chance of a proper overhaul and refit. The Ministry of War Transport would pay for the repair of the wear and tear of the war years to bring her back to her pre-war condition and John Brown's undertook to finish off those jobs interrupted by the liner's dash to a safe refuge. Cunard would pay for any extra work required to be done in addition to their original specifications.

One of the first jobs to be undertaken was to remove the de-gaussing coil and its protective steel-plate housing, to clear the hull ready for chipping and repainting. Wooden decks were replaced where damaged, panels smoothed down and repolished, kitchens refurbished and public rooms and cabins restored. Most striking of all, as the QE's battledress of grey was chipped away and the hull given a coat of anti-corrosion paint, the liner was gradually painted (in stages from stem to stern) in gleaming Cunard colours: black hull, brilliant white superstructure and that marvellous deep orange funnel colouring surrounded by a broad black top with two thin black bands on the orange/red of the lower funnel. Thirty tons of paint was used in the restoration.

Two thousand portholes were also scraped clean of grey paint; four thousand miles of electrical cabling was checked, tested and renewed where necessary. Deep down in the ship firebricks were replaced in the boilers and thousands of turbine blades were surveyed.

Just abaft the bridge a structure, looking rather like a water-tower, was removed. This, as on the *Mary*, had contained an early type of radar equipment, amongst the first to be fitted to merchant ships.

To achieve all this restoration work two thousand 'Bankies' had to be ferried out to the ship as she lay at the Tail along with all the equipment and materials that they needed.

The refit was not free from labour troubles. As the *Queen Elizabeth* would finally be fitted-out with her furnishings in Southampton the Scottish joiners reckoned that they should be paid at the same rate as their Southern counterparts. Cunard resisted the idea on the supposition that other unions would expect similar treatment. Another result would be detrimental increases in the cost of future new buildings.

The man directly in charge of the massive job of reconditioning the *Queen* was Shipyard Manager William McFarlane. He had been in a similar position during the construction of the *Mary* and would also oversee the post-war reconditioning of the elder ship in Southampton on her release from government service.

To further the completion of the *Elizabeth* he later came south to supervise the final stages of her restoration. The liner arrived back in Southampton on 16th June.

A thousand Clydebankers also came south to alleviate the acute shortage of local skilled labour. Two thousand people, all told, would be involved in the last, essential stages of fitting the *Queen Elizabeth* in her civilian finery.

During their stay in the south (a period which included the *Mary*'s refit between October 1946 and July 1947), the Scots were billeted in the hutments of Velmore Camp at Chandlers Ford. Each day they were bussed to and from the Docks by a fleet of thirty or so double-decker Corporation buses. One hundred female french polishers had also come south but they stayed nearer to the Docks, lodging in Portland Terrace near the city centre with its bombed Civic Centre.

The John Brown men were also entertained. On one occasion Dr. Horace King (the local Member of Parliament) and his concert party did the honours.

A flurry of criticism emanating from uninformed quarters of the country deplored the channelling of precious post-war resources and materials into the purpose of transporting a privileged few in luxury. The Times thundered to the rescue in defence of Cunard by reprinting its pre-war 'special' about the *Queen Elizabeth* which showed that the material being used in the liner had been in existence since before the war and that any new input into the liner using scarce post-war materials would be kept to a minimum.

The revitalizing of the *Queen* became the focal point of Britain's recovery from the human, material and financial ravages of war. She was the first British liner to be restored; she became, in essence, a Ship of State. She became 'The Wonder Ship'.

During her conversion for war the *Elizabeth* had undergone various refits to prepare her for troopship duties and unnecessary items of her peacetime outfit were removed and sent ashore. So it was that furniture and fittings from the liner found refuge in New York, Singapore and Sydney.

All these globally scattered fittings had to be brought to Southampton for refurbishment, assembly, sorting and fitting. The old *Aquitania* brought much of it from storage in New York directly to Southampton and those items stored in Sydney were returned via Liverpool where they were temporarily stored at Pilsworth in Lancashire. Fittings which had been intended for the *Queen* but had had their installation interrupted by the war had been stored at Brockenhurst and Lymington in the New Forest and at Woolston near Southampton for the duration of the war.

All the items were collated, processed and stored in two large aircraft hangars at Eastleigh on the outskirts of Southampton prior to being transported to the *Queen Elizabeth* and installed in their proper places as she lay alongside Berth 101.

Over 21,000 pieces of furniture were fitted into the liner. 4,500 settees, chairs and tables; 4,000 mattresses; 50,000 items of bed and table linen; 6,000 curtains which represented three miles of material; six miles or 2,000 carpets and rugs; and 1,500 wardrobes and dressing tables were included amongst the restored items.

Works of art were also renovated by the original artists and, in some cases, replaced where the original had 'disappeared' during her days as a troopship. The liner was also fitted with three radar sets of varying ranges, supplied by the electrical firm of Cossor.

On 7th August, the *Queen* went into the King George V dry dock, her entry being postponed for twelve hours because of strong winds.

Her 140 ton rudder was inspected (internally, as well as externally, as access doors had been built into the structure); propellers removed and cleaned; the underwater hull cleaned and painted; anchors tested; and each link of the anchor chain that had been spilled on to the dock bottom was tested and painted.

In total the reconversion had cost £1 million.

Sir Percy Bates visited the ship before she sailed from Southampton on 6th October once more for the Clyde for speed trials, adjusting her compass and testing other equipment at the Nab en route. Sir Percy told Commodore Bisset, retained after retirement to take the liner on her maiden voyage, that Her Majesty Queen Elizabeth would visit the liner at the Tail o' the Bank and remain on board for the measured-mile trials in the Firth of Clyde and that the maiden voyage had been arranged for 16th October.

Sir Percy added, 'We do not expect you to attempt to make speed records either on the trials or on the maiden voyage. The *Queen Mary* still holds the Blue Riband with her eastbound crossing in 1938 at 31.69 knots, and that is quite good enough! We shall be satisfied with crossings in four and a half days, more or less, according to the weather, at average speeds of from 27 to 29 knots, without driving the ships at their utmost speeds ....'

For the two *Queens* to race against one another would not only make commercial nonsense but it would also be a waste of fuel.

After the brief adjustments in the Channel the *Queen* headed north for the Firth of Clyde where she arrived three hours late because of fog early in the morning of 7th October. Sir James took his ship over the measured mile and satisfied himself that she could comfortably achieve 'over 30 knots without straining'.

Anchoring off Gourock at 11 am a party of distinguished guests came on board in readiness for the embarkation of the Royal party the next day. The guests included Sir Percy Bates and his wife; various Cunard directors – also accompanied by their wives; the Minister of Transport, the Right Honourable Alfred Barnes, and Mrs Barnes; Lord Aberconway, Chairman of John Brown Limited, and Lady Aberconway; and several senior officers and heads of departments of the Cunard White Star Line. These included G. M. Paterson, Naval Architect; J. Austin, Superintendent Engineer; and the Chief Marine Superintendent, Captain B.H. Davies. These men, amongst others, were on board to receive the thanks of country and company for the enormous amount of work and worry that they and their teams (probably all fuming because they had not been invited!) had put in to make the whole magnificent project possible.

The guests much admired the scale and detail of the finished liner as they toured the public rooms and peeked

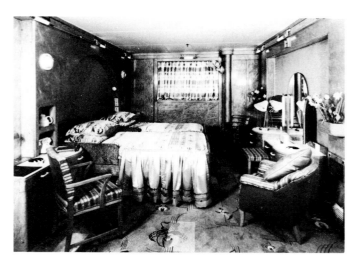

Over the period of refurbishment the liner's appointments were restored to the intended pre-war standards. This First (ex-Cabin) Class stateroom reflects the comfort to be found on board.

After the war rationing still continued in Britain so passengers were delighted to find articles freely available in the ship's shops that were as yet unobtainable or scarce in the mother country.

Both photos The University Archives, the University of Liverpool

into cabins. They admired the marquetry, the polish, the carpets and the feeling of freedom and peace not experienced for many years, all beautifully embodied in this symbol of Britain's determination to win the peace as well as the war.

Sir Percy Bates went ashore the next morning to meet the Royal Party at the start of a carefully timetabled day.

On board, the Commodore, noticing Doctor Maguire's white gloves, realised that he did not possess a pair, so the doctor gave his to Sir James. Lionel Carine, the purser, then gave one of his gloves to the doctor and hoped that nobody would notice that they were holding only one glove each!

The restored First Class Restaurant on 'R' deck.

After disembarking from the Royal train at Greenock Station at 10.30 am, the Queen and her two daughters, Elizabeth and Margaret Rose, were escorted to the gangway of the Clyde steamer *Queen Mary II* laying alongside Prince's Pier. Sir Percy Bates met the Royal party at the foot of the gangway and the ferry's skipper, Captain McGlasham, received the expanded party at the top.

As the ferry pulled away the Queen, responding to the cheers of the crowd of spectators on the pier, asked that the steamer be turned round to make a second pass by the pier to give the loyal Scots a better view of 'their' Queen.

During the short trip out to the liner Sir Percy showed Her Majesty the portrait of H.M. Queen Mary that was hung in the tender's lounge. This portrait had been presented by Cunard–White Star as a token of appreciation for the small ship giving up her name in favour of the mighty *Queen Mary*, then building on the Clyde. The smaller vessel then took on the suffix II.

The *Queen Mary II* arrived at the *Queen Elizabeth*'s anchorage and circumnavigated the huge liner which loomed above the smaller vessel.

The Chairman then led the Royal party on to the larger ship and presented the Commodore to his Royal guests. 'I have been looking forward to this moment so much' the Queen told Sir James. 'I have been watching the ship with great interest throughout the war.' The Commodore then presented his senior officers to the Queen who had a few words with each. The party then proceeded to the Promenade Deck where the Queen and the Princesses showed a great deal of interest in the names and initials that had been carved into the handrails by hundreds of GI's.

Commodore Bisset excused himself and disappeared to the Bridge while the Queen and the two Princesses were introduced to the Cunard Directors and other guests. A tour of the ship's main public rooms was then undertaken.

Meanwhile the liner, dressed overall and with the Royal Standard fluttering at her foremast head, weighed anchor and proceeded out to sea at 11.15.

Three quarters of an hour later Captain Wood, the Staff Captain, introduced H.M. the Queen to a group of the ship's leading ratings: Messrs Frogatt (Bo's'n), Mitchell (Carpenter), Kapper (Engine room Storekeeper), McAteer (Electrical Attendant), Evans (Chief Bedroom Steward) and Mrs Kilburn (Chief Stewardess) were all presented.

Danny McAteer, although described in the day's printed programme as an 'Electrical Attendant' preferred to refer to himself as a greaser, had been 'scrubbed and polished' by his mates with whom he was very popular and then given a tot of rum and a peppermint!

Commodore Sir James Bisset carefully watches a lifeboat drill. This rare photograph, although undated, could have been taken *en-route* between the Clyde and Southampton after the major post-war refurbishment.

Queen Elizabeth Historical Society

On being presented to the Queen he was so overcome that he could only stand there with tears in his eyes, so struck dumb by the occasion that he could not reply to Her Majesty's gentle questions.

The *Elizabeth* passed by the islands of Great and Little Cumbrae at 12.15, by which time her speed had been increased to 20 knots. By now the Queen and her daughters were freshening up in specially prepared suites on the Main Deck before taking cocktails (for the Queen) and lunch.

During luncheon the small island of Pladda at the southern tip of Arran appeared two miles to the north. Ten minutes after lunch, at 2.20 the liner began working up to 30 knots.

Lunch was followed by a short tour of the kitchens. Then, after another brief respite in their suites, the Royal family were escorted to the Bridge at 2.50 pm.

The two Princesses were each given a stop watch to time the liner's speed over the Measured Mile, (the mile was actually a two mile course with each mile marked out). The liner had by now been worked up to the desired speed. The Commodore explained to the party that he was not attempting to ascertain the liner's full speed but wanted to see what she could do with 175,000 h.p.

At 3 pm the *Queen Elizabeth* commenced her northward run in the brilliant sunshine and she covered the first mile in 2 minutes 1.3 seconds which gave a speed of 29,71 knots. The third marker was reached in 2 minutes 1.0 seconds, giving a speed of 29.75 knots.

The ship, completing her first run, turned in a great circle before heading on a southward course over the Measured Mile(s).

During the two minutes exactly that the liner took to cover the first part of the course (the second part of the course could not be accurately timed as the sun was reportedly so bright the mark on the second leg could not be taken), the Queen was invited to take the wheel under the guidance of Commodore Bisset who explained that the 140 ton rudder was controlled so precisely that the slightest movement of the wheel would affect the ship's course. After remarking how easy the wheel was, Her Majesty teased the Commodore 'You know, Commodore, I don't believe this wheel is really steering the ship at all.'

She then handed the wheel back to Quartermaster Campbell: 'I hope I am giving the ship back to you in good condition.'

On completion of the trials the Queen again toured the liner visiting the First Class Library (pre-war Cabin Class had now been renamed First), Observation Lounge, Gymnasium, Squash Racquet Court, First Class Swimming Pool, Turkish Bath and Doctor Maguire's Hospital.

A small crowd of crew members had gathered in the corridor and, as she left the Hospital, the Queen made straight for the group, chatting freely with them.

Meanwhile, after the speed runs, the Princesses had donned blue dust coats and gone down to the Engine Room where they were shown the machines by Chief Engineer John Swanson who had been on the vessel during her secret dash to New York.

Princess Elizabeth showed a special interest in the machinery as she had been a proficient motor mechanic during the war.

The *Queen Elizabeth*'s speed had been reduced to 25 knots after the trials and a course was set to take her back to the Clyde.

At 3.50 pm the huge steamer once again passed the Cumbraes at 20 knots on the inward journey and once again the Royals retired to their various suites until the liner anchored at 5 pm.

By 5.30 pm tenders had come alongside to take off the distinguished visitors and the smiling Queen gave that famous wave of her hand as she and the Princesses left the ship before returning to Balmoral.

Arriving at Southampton from the Clyde prior to her maiden voyage the *Queen Elizabeth* is about to pass the Royal Pier. Shortly afterwards she will pass the *Queen Mary* still in her battledress of grey, seen in the distant Western Docks.

Stewart Bale Ltd/Queen Elizabeth Historical Society

The next day four hundred guests embarked for a festive journey south to Soutnampton and, after bidding farewell to the Clyde, the *Queen* sailed at 8 pm.

In the Irish Sea a small coastal collier was seen wallowing along at all of 6 knots. The small vessel's skipper hoisted a flag-signal:

'What ship is that?'

As required by law the Commodore obligingly raised the Cunarder's recognition flags 'GBSS'

The floodlit *Queen Elizabeth* docked in Southampton at 11 pm on 10th October. The passengers landed – except for one man apparently ill in his stateroom. Surgeon Maquire was summoned and gave the Commodore his diagnosis: 'He'll be all right tomorrow. He's suffering from blood in his alcohol stream!'

The next day Sir Percy Bates and Sir James Bisset entertained to lunch on board many members of Parliament from both Houses including the Lord Chancellor and the Speaker of the House of Commons. Alan Patrick Herbert, writer and poet, was also invited. Already booked for the maiden voyage he had written a poem in readiness for the occasion: 'Bon Voyage.

'At last young giant, infant of the fleet,

Your medals on, you sail down Civvy Street:
And may you serve the peaceful folk you bring
As well, as nobly, as you served the King!
Here come your passengers; but who will check
The ghosts of soldiers crowding on your deck?'

Another writer summed up the impact that the *Queen* was making on a war-torn Britain (about to face several more years of hardship and rationing) when he wrote of the ship:

'... gleaming like a yacht, vast like a city, towering over the dockside in her enormous grace ... Where once she was grey and secret, now she is carnival with lights. Where once she was stark and stripped, now she is gay and opulent with the warm extravagance of luxury. She is the ultimate in liners, the greatest ship in the world!'

Stocked with food and cigarettes that, being unobtainable in Britain, had been brought over from the States on the ever-faithful *Aquitania*, the *Queen* was ready for her symbolic debut, tangible proof that 'Britain Can Make It' (the name of a manufacturing and trade exhibition that would show the world that the country was now ready to 'win the peace'). But before the liner sailed the Cunard–White Star Line would suffer an unhappy loss.

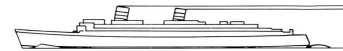

Chapter Eight

"…. Thank You to This Englishman."

The *Queen Elizabeth* was about to depart on her maiden voyage becoming as she did so the first British liner to be both reconverted from war duty and the first to start a regular post-war passenger service.

Among the first to board the liner in readiness for this gala occasion were the well-known British band leaders Bert Ambrose and his wife; Geraldo and his wife; Mr and Mrs Jack Hylton; and the singer Miss Frances Day (she had been on the maiden voyage of the *Queen Mary*).

On Tuesday 15th October 1946, six boat-train specials (drawn by a 'Merchant Navy' – class locomotive) left London's Waterloo Station bringing Tourist Class passengers down to Southampton.

The following day was sailing day and Sir Percy Bates was due to witness the departure from Waterloo of the 10.15 am Pullman Boat Train taking First Class passengers to the ship. Pulled by another locomotive of the 'Merchant Navy' class and appropriately named 'Cunard–White Star', the locomotive was fitted with a special headboard declaring 'RMS *Queen Elizabeth*'.

In all 2,228 passengers had booked for this prestigious premier voyage including some whose original booking for the ill-fated maiden voyage of 1941 had been cancelled.

But the plans of Sir Percy Bates were brought to an unexpectedly tragic end.

Suffering a heart attack, he had collapsed in his office on the day before the eagerly awaited sailing. His passage on the liner was cancelled (as was his wife's) and his luggage was taken ashore.

An announcement later appeared in the The Times (Thursday): 'On 16th October, at Hinderton Hall, Neston, Cheshire, Sir Percy Elly Bates, 4th Baronet, G.B.E. Greatly loved and loving husband of Mary Bates, aged 67 years. Funeral, Chidwall tomorrow (Friday) at 12 noon. No flowers, by request.'

On the very eve of the maiden voyage the cup of success had been dashed from the hands of the man who had made a long-cherished dream become a reality.

News of the chairman's death reached those on board by mid-morning and contrasted sharply with the high feeling of celebration that pervaded the liner, dockside and town.

Sir Percy's successor as chairman, his brother Fred Bates, requested that the company's houseflag flying at the liner's masthead should not be lowered to half-mast as would normally be expected in such circumstances. Commodore Bisset concurred, saying that the late chairman, whom he admired greatly both as a businessman and a gentleman, would not have wished anything should mar the gala occasion.

However, Sir James said that he would hold an onboard service at the same time as Sir Percy's funeral. Southampton Corporation recognised the honour that Sir Percy's vision had bestowed upon their town and the flags at the Civic Centre were flown at half-mast in his memory.

As the sailing of the *Queen Elizabeth* signalled the beginning of a new era of peace, so another occurrence signalled the end of an era of evil that, in a long career of crime, had sought the *Queen*'s destruction. This was the suicide in his Nuremberg cell of Hermann Goering, erstwhile Reichsmarshal and henchman of the megalomaniacal architect of Nazism whose ego had destroyed Germany.

Among the passengers embarked for the maiden voyage (the escape to New York in 1940 was denied by Cunard as being a 'maiden voyage' – the ship was merely moving from one berth to another while still under construction!) were many distinguished people, eminent personages in the worlds of government, diplomacy, the arts and society.

Sir Hartley Shawcross, the British Attorney General and recent Chief Prosecutor at the Nuremberg trials of Nazi war criminals, was sailing with the ship.

Sir Percy Elly Bates, chairman of Cunard-White Star and mastermind of the creation of the two *Queens*.

Helena Rubinstein, queen of the cosmetics world, was on board and Ludwig Bemelmans, distinguished journalist of The New Yorker and ardent Atlantic traveller also graced the passenger list. Amongst the politicians on board U.S. Senator Conolly was returning from the Paris Peace Conference and the Czech M. Jan Masaryk was travelling in his official capacity to a meeting of Foreign Ministers to be held at the United Nations. The British Secretary of State for Air, Philip Baker, was perhaps interested in comparing sea travel with the still infantile air route across the Atlantic.

Two unpublicised passengers came aboard the ship just before sailing time. Their arrival was surrounded by such a high degree of security that passengers' visitors were not allowed on board for the *de-rigeur* bon-voyage parties.

The first was U.N. bound Soviet Foreign Minister M. Molotov. 'I have great admiration for this great ship,' he

Wrapped against the early autumn chill of the North Atlantic, First Class passengers relish the comfort of deckchairs during the maiden voyage.

Stewart Bale Ltd/Queen Elizabeth Historical Society

told the Commodore. He was accompanied by his comrade colleague Vishinsky.

Promptly at 2 pm under a grey sky but on a calm sea the *Queen Elizabeth* pulled away from the quayside. Lines of flags cascaded downwards at an angle from each masthead as the liner was coaxed into the River Test. In spite of the occasion no band played her away. The Docks and Marine Band had been cancelled because of the passing of Sir Percy Bates.

Seven tugs gently cajoled the *Queen* into the stream to escort her to where the Test blended with the River Itchen to form Southampton Water. The *Clausentum*, *Canute* and *Paladin* of Red Funnel and the *Sloyne*, *Gladstone*, *Wellington* and *Romsey* of the Alexander Towing Company Limited pulled, tugged and fussed about the liner until she was solidly pointing towards Calshot and the Isle of Wight.

Her departure certainly did not go un-noticed. Tens of cheering, waving thousands watched her glide down the Water and into the Solent. Passing the Calshot Spit lightvessel she followed the dredged channel between the Calshot and Brambles sandbanks as she turned first to starboard and then to port as she sailed by Cowes, alive with hundreds of sightseers and where the light caught her so well. Then past the headland of East Cowes with the turrets of Queen Victoria's beloved Osborne House peeping above the woodlands that cascaded down to the water's edge.

Passing through the waters of Spithead between Ryde and Portsmouth she exchanged signals with her Royal Navy namesake, HMS *Queen Elizabeth*, anchored in the resting place of naval ships since ancient days. During the war the two ships had met in the Red Sea and one of the famous

Passengers line the sun deck railings as the liner passes the Battery with the ever-impressive Manhattan skyline looming above it.   *The University Archives, the University of Liverpool*

stories of the sea had the then troopship signalling to the warship 'Snap!'

Escorting paddle steamers and myriads of other pleasure craft escorted her, ploughing the sea into white furrows. Low flying aircraft and a helicopter buzzed the liner as she in turn sounded her magnificent siren, a cloud of steam from the whistles on her forward funnel appearing seconds before that glorious, heart-stopping roar hit those on shore.

Sailing into the English Channel the liner headed straight for New York. This would mean missing a call at Cherbourg, but this was done on two counts: the French port was still in a state of disrepair and the *Elizabeth* was fully booked. Steaming in an arc well off the Isle of Wight she headed into the vast unpredictable expanses of the North Atlantic.

For two days the liner made good progress with a following easterly wind. M. Molotov visited the Commodore in his quarters where he was offered vodka. He gave the reply that would become well-known to the Western world over the next few years: 'No!' But, to another offer, 'Veesky? Yes! Very Good!'

Both men then visited the Bridge where Molotov took the wheel for a few moments.

On Friday the weather changed from the fine conditions experienced previously to a fierce north-westerly gale and a very rough sea and the ship slowed down to ride out the worst of the storm.

Commodore Bisset went ahead with the memorial service to Sir Percy Bates at 11 o'clock with many of the crew present and those passengers who wished to attend. He ordered that the ship's flag be flown at half-mast.

Sir James gave the address: 'Sir Percy Bates was mainly responsible for building two great vessels. He watched them grow from masses of steel plates and girders, children of his brain, lived for them, worked for them and, alas, died for them. He was a man of great integrity, strong purpose and sympathetic understanding. All who worked for him and with him felt that they had lost a firm valuable friend. He loved the sea, loved ships, and loved those who went down to the sea in ships and did business in great waters.'

The Commodore then read Tennyson's poem 'Crossing the Bar', which had moved him so much when it was read at the funeral of another Cunard skipper, Sir James Charles of the *Aquitania*. Sir James had died of a 'broken heart' as he arrived at Southampton before leaving his beloved ship for retirement. Sir Percy's favourite hymn 'Praise, My Soul, the King of Heaven' was also sung, accompanied by the ship's orchestra.

Passenger Sir Warren Fisher summed up the greater influence of Sir Percy's life, beginning with these evocative words: 'Our country may well say thank you to this Englishman...'

Because of a strike by tug-boat men in New York there was a possibility that the *Queen* would be diverted to Halifax. But perhaps because of his experience with Halifax in the past and of the prestigious nature of the maiden arrival of the first passenger liner to enter New York since the war's end, Sir James decided to head for his original destination and dock the *Lizzie* without tugs, if need be, as

the *Queen Mary* had done in pre-war days.

The *QE*'s reserve of power came in useful in making up the time lost by Friday's storm. Ironically, her speed had to be decreased to 10 knots as she approached the New England coast as otherwise she would have arrived too early.

4 days, 16 hours and 18 minutes after passing the Bishop Rock in the English Channel, the *Queen* steamed by the Sandy Hook light just before dawn. She had averaged 27.99 knots and the Commodore later told reporters that the vessel had 'Performed beautifully – just like a sewing machine.'

The day was, appropriately enough, Trafalgar Day – 21st October. The pilot boarded and, once in the Lower Bay, the *Lizzie* anchored off quarantine using her specially installed bower anchor.

She remained anchored for two hours during which time a reception committee came on board headed by New York's 'Official Welcomer'. A hundred and fifty reporters and photographers boarded (80 had travelled westwards with the liner including Jack Frost of the Telegraph) most of whom wanted to interview Molotov. His cabin proved to be too cramped for the press conference so he took his interviewers to the Sun Deck. Perhaps he wanted to see the Manhattan skyline as the ship approached it or perhaps he wanted to show off the ship which had impressed him so much.

Port officials also boarded but many of the immigration formalities had already been settled during the voyage: an officer had travelled with the ship processing around 1,600 documents a day.

The City of New York was delighted to receive the *Queen Elizabeth* on this her commercial debut as she represented, even more so than during the war, employment and profit for hundreds of its citizens, now and for the years to come.

Ships afloat and factories ashore joined in the cacophony of sound that greeted the blimp-escorted, flag-strewn liner as she passed through the confines of the Hudson River on a beautifully sunny morning. 83,000 tons of magnificent proof that the situation in Europe was about to return to normal, progressed regally towards Pier 90 where she docked just before 8 am.

Under heavy guard an unsmiling Molotov was one of the first to leave the ship, being met by an equally unsmiling Andrei Gromyko, then a young Soviet delegate to the UN.

One of the first to board the ship was the mayor of New York, Vincent Impellitteri.

Ten thousand people paid $1 each to tour the liner over the next few days, the monies going to British and American seamen's charities. Amongst the visitors were many ex-GI's who wanted to show their families where they had slept and ate during their transportation to the battle zones. A few even found their carved initials still intact in the teak railings.

The liner stayed in New York, replenishing her stores and entertaining many, for four days until the 5th when, at 6 am, she sailed, bound for England.

On this second leg of her maiden voyage she carried the first two stowaways of her career. The first, ex-GI

With Jersey City in the background the *Queen* is carefully guided into her berth at the end of her maiden voyage.
The University Archives, the University of Liverpool

Kingsley Foster, was eager to join his war-bride and baby in England; the second was a young Canadian, John Dick, who was eager, for some reason, to get a job in Manchester.

The Cunard tried to dissuade the passengers who wanted to contribute towards the two men's fares; they said it would encourage further such attempts in the future. But the passengers had their way although the two men concerned were locked up for a short while as the ship approached English shores.

The *Queen* made the return trip in 5 days 3 hours arriving in her home port at 2 am on the last day of the month.

Ten thousand pieces of luggage were unloaded and Sir James Bisset told a reporter from Southampton's own Evening Echo that the *Queen Elizabeth* could 'not possibly have begun life as a passenger liner under happier auspices'.

The next sailing from Southampton – on 6th November, – set the seal on the liner's reputation as a favourite of the elite when the Duke and Duchess of Windsor sailed with the ship. They had embarked the evening before.

During this particular trip the Commodore conducted Divine Service, as was the usual practice when a Sunday was spent at sea.

The Duke and Duchess were in the congregation and as Sir James began to read Psalm 146 he realised that a particular passage might cause Britain's ex-King, and the woman for whom he had given up his throne, some embarrassment:

'O, put not your trust in princes, nor in any child of man: for there is no help in them!'

Reporters on board cornered Sir James after the service and asked him whether the inclusion of that particular Psalm had been intentional. The Commodore replied in the negative and it took all his powers of persuasion to dissuade the newspapermen from reporting the incident.

As the year grew old, so the liner's honeymoon with the Atlantic came to an end as the winter season brought forth its usual breed of storms.

A particularly stormy encounter with the ocean occurred at the beginning of December 1946. Forty-foot waves left four passengers with broken limbs and twenty-two others with lesser injuries.

But as the liner passed the Bishop Rock on the evening of Tuesday 3rd, a baby daughter was born to Mrs Joan Toley. Commodore Bisset christened the baby a few hours later – Elizabeth Dawn.

The *Queen* would encounter many storms during her voyage – especially during the winter months – and it would not be until the mid-fifties that anything would be done to alleviate the problem.

In the first few months of the *Elizabeth*'s service – up until the end of 1946 – the liner crossed the Atlantic nine times and carried a total of 11,000 passengers westward and 9,000 east to Europe.

Her popularity for the years to come was assured.

Chapter Nine

A Large Withdrawal From The Bank!

ommodore Bisset retired from the Cunard in January 1947, handing over command of the world's largest liner to Captain Charles Ford.

Tall and imposing, Captain Ford had commanded the *Elizabeth* on several occasions during the war, substituting for the Commodore as relief captain whilst the latter went ashore on leave.

Captain Ford would eventually be dubbed 'Foggy Ford' by his crew; ships which he commanded encountered

Staff Captain Thelwell was on the bridge with 'Foggy' Ford and as they approached the shores of the Isle of Wight, Thelwell said: 'I take a bet that none of the appropriate pilots are available'.

On arriving at the Nab the liner was slowed to pick up her pilot and, as the Staff Captain had guessed, it was not her usual pilot, Captain Bowyer, who stepped on board but a substitute, F.G. Dawson.

Although having spent many years with Trinity House

RMS *Queen Elizabeth* outward bound down Southampton Water having just passed the River Hamble and Warsash.

Author's collection

fog in New York on no fewer than thirteen consecutive occasions!

Three months after taking over command of the *Queen Elizabeth* Captain Ford faced an entirely different problem, one that could have finished his career at sea as well as his ship. Leaving the French coast on 14th April 1947, the liner headed towards Southampton – and home – with 2,246 passengers on board.

Unfortunately a thick fog lay on the channel and visibility was down to almost zero.

as a pilot, Dawson had no experience of handling ships as large as the *Queens* which was why Cunard had their chosen pilots to do the work. (Captain Bowyer had previously taken another ship out and had been unable to return to his station because of the weather.)

During the day the troopship *Ranchi* had had to anchor three times in the fog while trying to navigate the Solent and a small Panamanian collier, the *Georgic* of 6,000 tons, had gone aground off St. Catherine's Point at the southern tip of the Isle of Wight.

Above: Watching the attempts to free the grounded *Queen* hundreds of spectators on the surrounding shorelines had their last view of the liner just before a mist obscured the moment of victory. *Frank O. Braynard collection*

Left: Surrounded by tugs and lighters the *Queen Elizabeth*'s bows remained embedded in sand for many hours.
"The Wonderful Story of the Sea"

As the *Queen* progressed through Spithead the fog thinned and a late afternoon sun began to shine through the remaining haze.

Off Cowes the *Elizabeth* turned to starboard to bring her into the Thorn Channel, dredged between the Brambles and Calshot sandbanks.

Senior First Officer Geoffrey Marr – having changed into his shore clothes (other than for his uniform jacket, navy-blue raincoat and cap) – was at his docking post on the after docking bridge.

When the liner was halfway between her first turning point off Cowes and the second at Calshot that would bring her into the entrance of Southampton Water, Staff Captain Thelwell asked the officer of the watch: 'How's it going?' 'About halfway to Calshot lightvessel', came the reply.

From his post aft, Geoffrey Marr saw that the liner was far from safe. Looking forward along the whole length of the ship – which gave him a good idea of how well she was swinging – he could see that the ship, travelling at around 6 to 8 knots, was not keeping to the designated

The operational headquarters of the *Lizzie* – her Bridge. Full of gleaming brass, copper, white enamel paint and varnish this small area experienced many anxious moments. Note the four telegraphs – one for each Engine Room.

Collection of Louis O. Gorman/Queen Elizabeth Historical Society

channel. This fear was confirmed when the liner passed a buoy on the wrong side.

On the bridge the Captain voiced his own fears: 'I don't think we'll make the West approach channel, Pilot. She's turning too slowly.'

The pilot reassured the captain that all was well and continued to navigate the ship.

Suddenly the Captain ordered 'half astern on the starboard engines!' (the liner's port and starboard engines were used to help manoeuvre the ship on difficult bends), but it was too late.

Meanwhile, eighty feet below the bridge, a small motorboat – the *White Lady* out of Cowes – was bobbing around on the Solent.

Archie and Beatrice Turner (of the 'Mayflower' public house in the Island yachting and shipbuilding town) had decided to take their daughter Patricia and some friends out to see the *QE*'s arrival at close quarters instead of from the seafront at Cowes, always a vantage point from which to watch ships passing to and from Southampton.

Whilst waiting at what Archie Turner considered to be a safe point off Calshot, he and his companions were concerned to witness the huge liner practically cut across the bows of their launch.

This experience, frightening in itself, was followed by the *QE* gently coming to a halt. As she did so the occupants

of the motor-boat heard a loud crashing noise as giant propellers thrashed the shallow water into billowing clouds of yellow and black as sand and mud were churned up from the sea bed.

On the Bridge of the liner there was the faint sensation of a slight, lurching jolt which some on board never even felt. The ship shuddered slightly as the forward momentum of the vessel slowed and pushed the bows deeper into the mud.

Somebody said 'We're aground.'

The first indication that many on board had of the grounding was that the shoreline bordering the Solent had stopped 'moving'.

The gentleness of the sensation of grounding also seemed to decrease the further down in the ship that one was sited. On watch in the engine room the Second Engineer remembered a loud scraping noise as the liner dug her nose deeper into the gravel.

The Captain ordered 'Reverse engines' – but to no avail; the liner would not budge. To avoid sucking silt into the underwater inlets the engines were stopped until help became available.

Underwater the *Lizzie* was embedded in mud to a point just below the bridge.

By coincidence she had grounded in almost the same geographical spot that the *Aquitania* had done so, ten years previously almost to the day.

A signal for assistance was sent and – within an hour – company, port and salvage officials were aboard and in conference with the captain.

The tender *Romsey* which had brought the officials out to the stricken ship tried, meanwhile, a solo attempt at pulling the liner off the bank – but the towing line parted under the unequal strain.

By six the next morning, thirteen tugs had arrived from Southampton, Portsmouth Dockyard and Poole and were made fast using the liner's manila ropes. With two tugs in tandem on some of the ropes which were attached to the liner's seven after bollards the first attempt to release the liner from the grip of the mud was made.

Water ballast had been pumped overboard to lighten the ship forward and to lift her bow; little oil remained to be removed after the transatlantic journey, but a barge arrived alongside to take it off if necessary.

The salvage attempt at the first available high tide failed and the *Elizabeth* had to wait until the next day when another suitable tide would occur.

The second attempt at salvage was directed once again by signals given on the liner's whistles with toots of acknowledgement blown in response by the tugs.

With twelve tugs on the ropes and two more tugs on each side of the liner, she was pulled first to port for fifteen minutes, then, on a signal, to starboard for a similar period, thus waggling the ship in slow motion like a giant tooth waiting to be pulled. The treatment worked as a slight movement could be felt as the restraining grip of the mud's suction was broken.

At 8.40 pm on the evening of Tuesday 15th April, with an increasing fog which gradually obscured the lovely evening light that had hitherto illuminated the scene, and on the third 'waggle' the ship's engines joined in the struggle. The ship slid out of her temporary prison, dark smoke streaming from her funnels.

Amidst the cheers from those on board, the liner's freed bows were taken into control by the tugs which had hurriedly scampered forward.

Hearing the whistle booming out from the liberated liner, cheers also went up from the crowds on shore. Thousands of sightseers lined the shore at Calshot, many coming from miles away in coach specials, to see the spectacle; amongst the crowd was retired Chief Engineer John Swanson who thoroughly enjoyed the excitement – and told the Echo's reporter so!

Two more blasts on her whistles indicated that the liner was under her own power but, because of the fog, the spectators on shore could only guess that she was not going to try to reach Southampton that night. They were right; the liner replenished her ballast and retraced her wake of twenty six hours previously, anchoring overnight a few miles away to the south in Cowes Roads.

The next morning she steamed into Southampton – fifty hours late!

A lot of baggage had been sent ashore during the attempt to lighten the ship and her First Class passengers had also been disembarked at 4 pm on the 15th via two local paddle steamers – the *Solent Queen* of Red Funnel and Southern Railway's *Merstone*.

Amongst the First Class travellers were the Duke of Marlborough, Lady Peel (better known as Bea Lillie, the film actress), playwright Terence Rattigan and Randolph Churchill – journalist and son of Britain's victorious wartime leader.

Bea Lillie had been photographed waving obligingly over the ship's side during the period of grounding by an enterprising photographer who had worked his way on to one of the tugs. But Randolph Churchill had no reason to be cheery. He was furious!

As an 'on the spot' journalist his opportunity of a 'scoop' on a story that would make headlines had been thwarted.

After the grounding Churchill found his way to the Bridge – the 'holy of holies' where passengers were definitely not allowed – but Captain Ford refused to give him an interview. Churchill was just 'another passenger' – as far as the captain was concerned – who might just get in the way at that particularly worrying time.

But, in spite of being gently 'warned-off' even by the Staff Captain, the journalist was not to be deterred, He tried once more – and then again as his newspaper clamoured for a story.

Randolph Churchill's frustration was aggravated even further when the radio room was closed down on orders soon after the grounding and his telegram was refused acceptance. This 'unwarranted censorship' that one would have expected only under wartime conditions was later lifted but, even then, only short messages were accepted. Even so, the telegram of one passenger that described the *Elizabeth* as being 'stuck' had the offending word changed to 'delayed'.

The problem of communication was further exacerbated by the ship not having a tannoy system. Passengers were not kept officially informed as to what was happening and many only received information – usually rumour – gleaned from individual crew members.

The day following the *Lizzie*'s delayed but jubilant arrival into Southampton, divers inspected the underwater hull for signs of damage.

Other than for silt found in some inlets there was very little evidence of the grounding. A fifty foot length of one-inch rope was also found to be coiled around a propeller, but otherwise nothing untoward was found in connection with the episode.

Internally the condensers and oil coolant inlets were cleared of shells and gravel but other than having her dignity affronted the *Queen* had come through her ordeal relatively unscathed.

She had however, been entered onto Lloyd's casualty list after refusing to accede to the tugs' first attempts to secure her release. Her hull, machinery and fittings were insured for just under £6 million, with a further value of £255,000 placed on her cargo and the announcement of her grounding was given 'star billing'.

But her reputation was undamaged and ten years of popularity and profit were set to follow.

Chapter Ten

Jobs, Yarns And Cabin 52

The *Queen Mary*'s post-war refit in Southampton was completed and, on 1st August 1947, she joined her larger sister to commence the long delayed two-ship Atlantic express ferry service for which they had both been built.

The size, chic and romance of the two beautiful liners (combined with their heroic reputations and Cunard's publicity campaigns) would ensure that the liners would be well patronised, especially during the calmer summer months.

Commodores of the Cunard Line (but other than for Sir James Bisset and Sir Ivan Thompson, none had been bestowed with the knighthood that had been more-or-less customary before the war) – flew their flag on the company's flagship, the largest liner the world had ever seen. A relief captain, the 'bagman', would also act as relief for the captains of the *Queens* and *Mauretania*, the latter ship also acting as a substitute for whichever *Queen* was undergoing refit in dry-dock.

From Townley at the very beginning to Marr at the very end, a succession of skippers had made the 'Waterloo Elm' lined Captain's day-room their home. Caunce, Cove, Divers, Ford, Grattidge, Jones, MacLean, Morris, Snow, Sorrel, Thelwell, Thompson, Watts and Williams were amongst those who had enjoyed sovereignty over a mobile, thriving city of several thousand people. It was a combined hotel, town-hall and factory with the passengers as the guests, the captain and his staff as the management and administrators and the crew seeing to the needs of all those on board.

The 'municipal and industrial' employees under the captain's command changed with the years but a large proportion of the crew had made the sea, the *Queens*, their lives. Indeed, so jealously guarded were the prestigious and respected positions on the *Queens* that sons would find employment on board on the recommendation of their fathers.

During almost two decades following the end of the war, young men in Britain were 'called up' for two years' National Service in the armed forces. An alternative was the option to serve in the Merchant Navy (a vital task during conflict) and the prospect of earning £2 a week in the forces or to be well-paid in the merchant service proved to be a one-sided choice for many youngsters.

Some of the captains of the *Queens* would ultimately write their autobiographies giving accounts of life in perhaps the most famous – certainly the most glamorous – job in the world.

But as not much has been set down about the shipboard lives of other members of the crew, it may be useful to redress the balance – even if briefly.

The hotel staff, as they became known, included bedroom stewards, stewardesses and restaurant stewards – generally known as the waiters. These groups, having direct access to the passengers, were able to make a very lucrative living by supplementing a basic wage with the tips proffered by their well-attended charges, some of whom were generous in their làrgesse – some less so.

For their part the steward was expected, at the end of each voyage, to tip those who in turn supported him in the performance of his duties.

A bedroom steward for example would tip – perhaps £1 each – the linen keeper who provided him with fresh sheets, pillow-cases etc. for his cabins; the larder cook with whom he came to an agreement to feed him during the voyage (meals were taken anywhere convenient and usually eaten standing up as no special messes were available for stewards); he would also tip the 'Glory Hole' steward for waking him each morning and for making his bed (this janitor might serve 4 to 5 dormitories each sleeping 12 to 18 men each of whom would give him a similar tip), and so on.

A restaurant steward would also find tips were expected by the kitchen staff and storemen who provided him with the means for carrying out his duties.

Appointed Staff Chief Engineer of the *Lizzie* in 1964 and Chief Engineer in 1967, Stanley Tattershall had previously served in many of the company's ships.   *R. Bruce Grice*

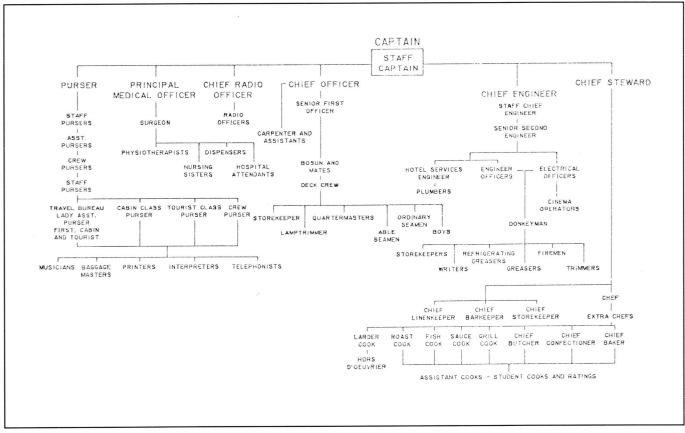

The staff 'family tree' of the *Queen Elizabeth*.   *Cunard/Gary Smith*

If a steward was inclined to be too covetous of his tips then he soon found that the enthusiasm of his back-up team fell away!

Tipping oiled the cogs of a well-run machine; it was the lifeblood of an efficient service. Passengers and crew alike were either 'good bloods' if they tipped well or 'bad bloods' if they did not.

The stewards and other ship's personnel dined on the same fare as the passengers and palates soon become bored with succulent roasts, etc. On making representations to the staff captain a quantity of corned beef was obtained but this somehow found its way to the officers' and pursers' tables. Not until the advent of the *QE2* would proper messes be provided with the 'home cooking' that the crew yearned for.

Through the infra-structure of the *Queens* a man could avail himself of a training that would stand him in good stead should he decide to leave the sea and set up business on shore. To have been a first class Cunard steward was in itself an assurance of excellence, and many such men still thank the Cunard for the experience received.

From bell-boy to Chief Bedroom Steward, there was a steady progression for the right man.

A young boy of fourteen years of age and of less than 5 foot in height (this height requirement was later changed as the school leaving age was increased to 15) could join the company as a bell-boy, undergoing eight weeks' training at the Sea School at Gravesend (usually during the liner's eight week annual winter lay-up and overhaul).

When the *Queen Elizabeth* first sailed after the war the bell-boys had been fitted with tailored uniforms of powder blue with silver piping; the uniform was later changed to maroon. A pill box hat (sometimes useful as an improvised football) was attached to a button on the jacket, and a loop was provided for the stowage of white gloves.

Rising at 5.30 am the boys would be given half- an-hour's PT on the Sun Deck followed by a quick cup of coffee and a change into uniform before breakfast at 7.20. The boys then lined up for inspection on 'R' deck which required personal cleanliness and a smart appearance.

Then it was time to start the day's various duties. A favourite was manning the doors to the First Class Restaurant as tips gleaned per voyage could be in the region of $200 to $300. One of the least popular assignments was duty in the Radio Room awaiting telegrams. Here tips were less frequent but on one west-bound trip a young bell-boy, James Collins (his autograph book always tucked into his tunic), was given a telegram – 'Deliver this to Bing Crosby'.

On its delivery the great singing star took the telegram from the silver tray, signed for it and said: 'Hang on, I've got something for you' and put $100 bill on the salver, the equivalent of several months wages.

A rise from bell-boy to commis waiter (assistant waiter) put a youngster on a course for gradual advancement. Waiters and bedroom stewards progressed upwards through Tourist, Cabin and First Class duties, gradually increasing their skills over the years until a top bedroom steward could be entrusted with his passengers' valuables and be relied on to perform discreetly any task demanded by his 'bloods'

A bedroom steward usually had a block of 44 passengers to look after in 2, 3 or 4 berth cabins.

On sailing days a passenger might hold a party in his or her cabin. Other than for delivering baskets of fruit or flowers (chocolate rabbits and eggs at Easter) to the cabin, the steward (or stewardess) might have to organise trays of canapes for the guests.

For these bon voyage parties Cunard would later find that they had to make a charge for their provisioning. Even so, it was reckoned that the number of parties being held decreased by only 25% from the usual two hundred or so before the charge was made.

It was not unusual for some well-wishers to celebrate a little too well and subsequently miss the last call for going ashore. The reluctant 'stowaway' might then have to be put off on to a tug or even on to the pilot vessel.

On board, some passengers could make difficult demands of their steward. Jim Jone recalls 'one well-heeled but ignorant' First Class passenger, the son of an eminent British jeweller, asking for a smoked salmon sandwich. Particularly difficult to cut in large slices smoked salmon was usually only used on canapes so the Chief Steward (who held the key to the cupboard in which the salmon was kept) asked Jim Jone 'Are you sure?' – 'Yes'. The cold-larder cook whose job it was to prepare the salmon was verbally colourfully less than receptive to the idea of having to slice such large portions.

But nothing was impossible in those days.

At the end of each trip the bedroom stewards would have to vacuum, polish and generally service the cabins in readiness for the next occupants. After each round voyage the portholes would be cleaned with brass rims being wire-wooled and polished to rid them of the effects of salt water. Other crew members who were not busy while in port might lend a hand for a $1 or so.

Accidents occurred at times, but one of the most amusing that happened on the *QE* occurred when a bedroom steward illegally emptied his vacuum bag through an open porthole.

Caught by the wind the contents of the bag were sucked into another open port serving one of the crews' toilets.

This was followed by a dust-covered and very irate chief bedroom steward emerging from the toilet spluttering and threatening vengeance on the perpetrator of the crime!

Part of a bedroom steward's duties was to clean the passageways outside the cabins under his charge. Kneelers and sponges had to be used for this job as the use of mops (sometimes bought ashore with the steward's own money) was considered a breach of discipline. Eventually the company relented and the 'undignified' kneelers were dispensed with.

A bell-boy's life at sea on a great liner could be rewarding in many ways. Here, young 15 year olds Jim Collins (left) and Kenny Ailing man the doors to the first class saloon.

James Collins

A trusted position to achieve was that of a first class bedroom steward. Jim Jone was one of the lucky ones. *Jim Jone*

A waiter, by the time he had progressed to the First Class Restaurant, was a man unequalled in his trade.

An expert at silver service, he could also carve a 40 pound turkey in five minutes, and joint a chicken into five portions in as many seconds! One of the more skilful jobs requiring much practice under expert supervision was to carve meat from the baron of beef contained within the 'Silver Bullet', a dome covered trolley wheeled from table to table in First Class. Cabin and Tourist classes had their meat ready served on a plate.

A waiter would also have other duties. Put in charge of condiments, napkins etc. he would be known as the 'Cruet King', 'Linen King', 'Fruit King' and so on.

Still in uniform, but in a party spirit, engineer Lovell Taylor 'lets rip' at one of the engineers' parties. *Lovell Taylor*

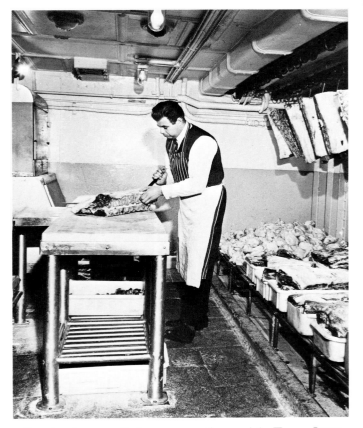

Catering for a small city was a continuous job. Trevor Jones prepares a side of beef for the following day meals.

R. Bruce Grice

It was a good lucrative life for many and one which was jealously guarded.

The crew who did not come into contact with the public were as proud of their jobs as those who did – even if they did grumble on occasion. But it seemed that every few years or so a bad element would manage to find employment on the *Queens* and the presence of such an individual or group of individuals could prove disruptive to the rest of the crew.

However, they were not tolerated and after an incident involving such a group, Commodore Marr refused to sail until the rough element was put ashore, in spite of union protestations.

These groups of men were known colloquially as 'Belfast Men' and once their games of 'Crown and Anchor' or other misdemeanours were discovered they received short shrift from the ship's Master-at-Arms and the company.

Off duty, the crew could fetch beer from the 'Pig and Whistle' and take it back to their 'Glory Hole' as the 'Pig' was not a very comfortable place in which to sit around: it tended to be draughty and the bench seats were hard.

Sometimes a singing star or comedian who was travelling as a passenger would come down to the 'Pig and Whistle' to entertain the crew. It was all summed up by Gracie Fields while travelling on the *Mary*: 'I'll sing f'lads f'nowt, but passengers can pay!'.

Ginger Rogers sang for the 'lads', as did Vera Lynn. Richard Burton and Alan Ladd drank with them. Comedian Frankie Howard gave a well-received performance and afterwards acknowledged the cheers with a deep bow, arm across waist. As he rose his arm waved in a rotating motion, fore and middle fingers extended in appreciation of his applauding audience!

Engineer Lovell Taylor (himself no mean trumpeter who enjoyed many a jazz-session on board) remembers Bob Hope going through his act for which Lovell formed part of the backing band. Lovell recalls:

'After a few bars of his signature tune 'Thanks for the Memory' Bob Hope starts off by saying:

'I've played in a lot of strange places in my time, but I've never played in a sewer before! Good evening rats!', and goes straight into one of his famous comedy routines. The crowds start roaring and stamping their feet, shouting for more'.

Bob Hope's act was followed by 'Jane', a crew member and one of the most famous amateur 'drag' artists afloat.

Of all the jobs on the ship, that of barman was perhaps one of the most lucrative. When on the rare occasion the job changed hands, it was accompanied by a covert payment of quite a large sum of money which, if they had been aware of the practice, those in authority would certainly have discouraged.

The seeking of this sought-after position came to an end when the Cunard complained that their profits from the bars were down. It transpired that the barmen had been buying their own cheaper liquor, keeping it under the bar and selling it in preference to the company's stock!

Even the customers of the 'Pig and Whistle' were not immune from 'private enterprise'. After a severe bout of sickness amongst the crew it transpired that plumbers had somehow managed to get sea water into fresh water pipes during a maintenance job. Unfortunately no one had told the 'Pig's' barman who had hitherto been regularly watering the beer.

Ready with help and a smile. The *Lizzie*'s hospital staff.

The University Archives, the University of Liverpool

One crew member slightly avenged his mates. He was in the habit of using an innocuous tin mug for his pint of beer which he duly passed over the bar to be filled. One day a pint glass was filled by mistake and, on being transferred to the tin mug, the beer disappeared to well below the rim. His 'pint' mug had held almost 50% more.

Perhaps the most neglected of all the ship's company – the engineers – lived in a world of their own. Completely detached from the cash flow circulating above they had a unique humour and culture, regarding the rest of their 'shipmates' with a 'mutual but friendly contempt'.

The *Lizzie* was generally a popular ship with the crew, being more modern and easier to work than the *Mary*, but she did not fully attain the affection that the latter ship enjoyed.

But, even so, the *QE* was not generally well-liked amongst her engineers.

This was due in the most part to her boiler rooms. Very hot with temperatures sometimes reaching 150°F the huge boilers had to be carefully balanced when in port.

Whereas the *Queen Mary* had three Scotch boilers that had been installed solely to provide power to the ship's hotel services, the *Lizzie* had to use two of her twelve Yarrow type boilers (larger than the 24 similar ones on the

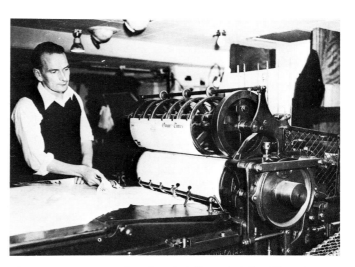

A newspaper was printed and delivered daily. The 'Ocean Times' succeeded the wartime 'The Elizabethan' in bringing the latest news.

The University Archives, the University of Liverpool

Above: World news, private messages, stock market prices, weather and company business were all received and sent from the Radio Room of the *Elizabeth*, call sign GBSS.

R. Bruce Grice

Left: Engineer and electrical officers during an evening in the Ward Room.

Lovell Taylor

A group of children in the play room with Helen Wiltshire.

Collection of Jim Jone

Mary) to perform the same function both at sea and in port.

This meant, in simple terms, that when the *QE* was due to sail or be docked, the other boilers had to be brought into or taken out of line with those already either under steam or 'cold', with a cross connection being made when pressures were equalised in all boilers.

Failure to ensure that the pressures were equal either way would lead either to a loss in pressure or blown safety valves!

Heating or shutting down the boilers was also a lengthy procedure. The *Mary*'s smaller boilers were very controllable and her engineers considered themselves unlucky if shut-down took more than an hour. But with a similar operation on the *Elizabeth* the larger boilers took anything from two and a half to four hours to perform.

Apart from the Staff Chief Engineer's frantic but futile efforts in trying to trace the origins of the aroma of baked potatoes ('Baked Idaho a'la Main Stop') cooking away on a piece of hot machinery in the Boiler Room, there are countless other more often than not humorous stories that tell of life down below.

The *Queen*'s position was often calculated by dead-reckoning and to do this the bridge would want to know the total engine revolutions as indicated by the Chadburn Counters sited on the Engine Room platforms below the board-mounted, brass-contained gauges.

The revolutions indicated by the counters did not always reflect the actual revolutions turned by the propeller shafts so the engineer on watch would sometimes use the palm of his hand to spin the counter round to obtain a more 'reasonable' reading.

On more than one occasion, after the removal of the cover plate and an application of an over-zealous hand, the counter wheels – plus various cogs and springs – scattered over the Engine Room platform floor!

(It was said of the Engine Room floor plates that the only decent de-greaser was locally brewed coffee!)

Six hours before sailing a warming through of engines would take place and, four hours later, the telegraphs and navigational equipment were tested, as were the ship's whistles. The engineers on watch gave a gradual feed of steam to the turbines. This was to prevent localised overheating on the turbine blades and was usually done by bleeding steam into the ahead and astern inlets of each engine, thus cancelling out any tendency to move.

However, on carrying out the exercise on one particular night, a few hours before sailing the next morning, the 2nd Engineer said to the Junior 5th: 'Do you know what that 'clunk' was?'

The 'clunk' turned out to be the gear-box coupling taking up the load and the accompanying, increasing 'whirring' noise meant that the engines had 'gone live'. The liner was underway whilst still tied-up at the quayside!

Before the engines could be disengaged the *Queen Elizabeth*'s stern had swung away from the quay sufficiently enough to dislodge one of the after storing conveyers that spanned the water between ship and shore leaving it suspended from the open cargo port.

Once the ship was at sea and on course the steering power could be reduced and one or two of the three pumps could be shut down to economise on power.

On one voyage, just after leaving Cherbourg, the duty engineer stopped the electric motor driving one of the steering gear pumps and inadvertently mechanically disconnected the servo control of a 'live' pump.

As soon as this happened the error of his ways was dramatically revealed as the counter-weight of the live – but now uncontrolled – pump took over as a constant hydraulic flow in one direction took place.

This had the effect of pushing the rams, and consequently the rudder pintle, into a maximum position.

The result was a surprise to several hundred unsuspecting people on the ship, not least of all those on the Bridge, as the *Queen* angled over into one of the tightest high-speed turns of her career. One can only guess at the chaos in the restaurants where havoc must have been wreaked on beautifully laid tables.

Ivan ('Jack') Horner was on his first trip on the *Lizzie* – a green, junior lubrication engineer in the aft Engine Room. After the ship had left Southampton he came on watch and read the report left on the blackboard by the previous watch.

The Cabin Class swimming pool had, unusually, been filled whilst crossing the Channel and, for safety reasons, it was required that it had to be pumped-out before the *Elizabeth* reached Cherbourg. It was Jack's job to see that this was done.

Unfortunately no one had told the engineer that the steam (that circulated between the pool's base and the structure beneath to warm the water) had also to be turned off.

It was not long before a frantic and almost unintelligible swimming pool attendant telephoned the engine room: 'The swimming pool's blowing up! There goes a tile .... there's another!' as tiles erupted in small explosions from the overheated floor.

A never ending job was the baking of fresh bread and rolls.
The original brick ovens lasted throughout the liner's life.
R. Bruce Grice

In the main kitchen Senior Chef Coward checks on the boiling
of a ham. *R. Bruce Grice*

Part of a greaser's job was to oil the many plummer
blocks that transmitted the thrust of the propeller shafts
into the forward or astern motion of the ship.

A few of these blocks were housed in the shaft tunnels
extending out of the ship's side, terminating at the
propellers. A very cramped space and, if an unwary greaser
leant too far over, the rotating shaft would catch him and
roll him over.

It was not unknown for the Engine Room to telephone
the Bridge for permission to stop one shaft in order to
retrieve a stranded – but wiser – greaser!

The more sociable of the engineers always enjoyed a
good party whether it was their own or somebody else's.

The pursers usually extended a token invitation to 'one
or two engineers' to attend their party but one day
somebody in the pursers' department made a mistake and
the invitation was addressed to 'The Engineers'.

As a consequence – and once it was known whisky was
to be provided as well as beer - the engineers arrived in
droves as they came off duty. The party was thus kept going
for hours, the whisky arriving by the box!

The engineers' cabins were sited on the Sun Deck
forward of the Verandah Grill, a lesson learnt from the
Mary where accommodation was originally sited near the
Engine Room. This had meant that the engineers did not
see much sunlight – as well as being disturbed by the noise
of the 'shop' when off duty – so additional accommodation
was built over the Verandah Grill during an early refit.

Some of the least popular engineers' cabins on the
Elizabeth were athwart-ships with the amidships expansion
joint in the corridor floor outside. When the ship was
'working' during rough weather the joint would noisily
creak away with each pitch of the ship's bow, keeping the
slumbering engineers within the affected cabins awake.

The engineers' own parties were held in one of their
cabins that became legendary (and notorious) – Cabin 52.

For some reason Cabin 52 was larger than most and
proved to be ideal for the influx of engineers and guests
that the parties attracted.

The ship's musicians were often invited to the gatherings, their music giving the proceedings an extra boost and,
sometimes, musically talented members of the Engineering
Department would join together to give an impromptu
jazz-session.

One particular party in the cabin lasted for almost
FOUR days with a change of personnel every few hours as
duty called some away and relief brought in new faces or
those who were returning for more.

The party came to an abrupt end when the Staff Chief
called on the participants '... to pack it in!'

As a postscript, a disgruntled party-goer crept into the
Staff's cabin at 4 am when the latter was asleep and acti-
vated a fire extinguisher. The doused 'Staff' swore that he
heard the sound of fleeing footsteps receding towards a
particular cabin. As a result three alleged culprits were
marched before the Staff Captain and were later transferred
to the *Mary*.

The real culprit, however, remained on the *Lizzie* until
he struck again: annoyed by a squeaking segregation gate

on the Sports Deck above him he hacksawed the offending item from its hinges and dropped the remains overboard.

He was soon apprehended because when he had collected the hacksaw with which to perpetrate the deed from a tool store he had signed for it in his own name!

A large storeroom also became another popular venue for crew gatherings. The room – normally used to store disassembled coffins – was rigged with coloured lights and other essential trappings and became known as 'The Coffin Club' entry to which was by specially printed membership cards.

Life for the crew on board of course was not a continuous succession of misdemeanours and parties although such incidents do provide many memories for some of the men who served on the *Queen Elizabeth*.

The passengers who filled the ship were, on the whole, unaware of the off-duty activities of the crew and the ship's reputation for efficiency and service remained unblemished. If they did know, then not a few smiles would have been raised.

Misfortune sometimes struck the liner and the crew, too, was not immune. On the morning of Trafalgar Day (21st October) 1953, during a routine lifeboat exercise in Southampton (that required selected lifeboats to be manned, lowered and raised again), number 26 boat was being retrieved from the water when it suddenly broke from its falls. As it fell it capsized, two men were catapulted into the sea and the falling boat collided with boat number 24, injuring the latter's tillerman.

Douglas Warsom, a twenty six year old waiter, dived from boat 24 and bravely rescued those who had fallen into the water. One of the men had received severe injuries and was later awarded £4,000 in compensation.

In spite of potential dangers the crew were always ready to enjoy themselves – even if a little foolhardily.

A young second Hors d'Oeuvrier, Martin Rowland, recalls one such incident that occurred during one of the *QE*'s cruising jaunts to the Caribbean during her twilight years:

Some of the crew had decided they would besport themselves with a little fishing. Attaching a ham to a meat hook which was connected, via a strong line, to a steam winch, their attempt at shark fishing was about to commence over the liner's stern. Before long one of these fearsome creatures was caught and the steam winch strained to haul it in. To prevent its anticipated thrashing on the after deck, a rather slow minded kitchen porter was attached to another rope and lowered over the side. His purpose was 'to clobber the shark with a club' before it could wreak havoc on board!

In their heyday the two *Queen*'s would spend two, three or four days in port during each turnaround. In Southampton this meant time at home with families or friends, but a similar time spent in New York might hang heavily once the excitement of being in that thriving city wore off after a few voyages.

However, many of the crew enjoyed a relationship with the city and its inhabitants. Many New Yorkers were enthraled by someone not only with an English accent but by one who also worked on the great liners.

Theatre, music and visiting American friends (perhaps made while on board) occupied the time of some, while others might be happy in buying $100 suits (ordered one trip and collected the next) that would impress the people at home.

Whilst in New York a crewman might find himself short of cash as, even after an allotment had been paid to his family, he was allowed to take only limited funds ashore.

A good method of obtaining money was to sell a pint of blood to a local hospital. One hospital gave $10 a pint but if the wrong establishment was chosen he would receive only an enamelled flag pin for his trouble.

Money could be made on board even in port. If the chance of winning the crew's own 'Nantucket Sweep' (the 'Nab Sweep' on the English side) was missed-where $1 bought a minute of an hour's estimated time that the ship would pass the sea mark ($1 per half minute in the similar Engine Room "Battery Sweep") – then a steward could act as a guide to eager American sightseers.

With twenty people in such a group each tipping $5 this could be a lucrative pursuit.

Whether or not the company approved was another matter as these guided tours could be expensive to the Line in terms of lost 'souvenirs'.

Apart from illegal dice games played furtively on board (or with dockers on either side of 'The Pond'), other, more imaginative, betting games were played.

One New Year's Eve found the *Queen Elizabeth* in New York so sixteen men joined in a $5-a-head race from the ship to the top of the Empire State Building with the winner taking all.

The crew also had their own benefit club into which anyone on board could pay one shilling (5p) a week. This donation entitled them to two pounds ten shillings (£2.50) a week for up to a year should they be unfortunate enough to be ill for that length of time.

Sports and social activities and interests were also encouraged on board. A special magazine, the '*QE*' was published and intership sports, such as the 'Atlantic Cup' for football, were hotly contested. Underprivileged children in Southampton were entertained during the winter overhaul with tea, American comics and a show, all paid for by the crew.

Whilst in New York some of the crew preferred to visit famous haunts such as 'Jack Dempsey's' or the 'Market Diner', an all-night establishment opposite Pier 90 and long regarded as a favourite of Cunard men.

Engineer Ian Baker recalls enjoying a drink with a friend in the 'Market Diner' when, looking out at the *Lizzie*, they saw that the liner was about to sail.

As they should have been on board they left their drinks, ran across the road, past a security guard and on to the Pier towards the last gangway.

The shouts of the security guard fell on deaf ears but the sound of gunshots and the sensation of bullets flying past them encouraged the two men to fall flat on the ground. The guard was then able to inspect their passes at ease!

Sometimes, as the *Queen Elizabeth*'s propellers started to churn up the murky riverbed ooze of the Hudson, a

Above: The starboard aft engine room platform showing ahead and astern manoeuvring valve control wheels, Bridge telegraph, Chadburn counter (to the left of the officer) and, to the right, the deck where the junior engineers wrote up their logs.
R. Bruce Grice

Left: A junior engineering officer tops-up one of the plummer blocks that transmitted the thrust of the propeller shaft into motion.
R. Bruce Grice

body, victim of murder or suicide, would float to the surface. One crewman recalls the gruesome sight of a New York policeman's body so appearing: the murdered man had disappeared several weeks previously.

The hygiene of foreign ships visiting their ports was a prime consideration to the American authorities and they were very conscientious in the performance of their duties.

On each arrival the 'Rat Man', as the crew called him, would arrive on board with his torch and mirror in readiness to inspect the *Elizabeth*'s kitchens. Heavy fines were liable should any food etc. be found under work benches. After one such complaint Cunard were requested that sills should be fitted over the spaces between bench and deck before the liner sailed.

This meant that deck tiling had to be chipped up, the sills fitted and then the tiles relaid.

The liner was also fined if she emitted too much smoke whilst in port. After receiving a vigorous telling-off for such a misdemeanour the Chief Engineer called his men up to his cabin so that he could pass on the admonishment he had received.

After doing so he must have felt sorry for the engineers standing before him, so he offered them a drink. Knowing that their chief was allowed a quota of spirits for which he did not pay, the men from the engine room asked for beer – for which he did! (Sailing across the Atlantic the Engine Room received a haughty call from the Bridge: 'Did you know there is black smoke coming from the funnels?' 'What colour did you expect it to be?' came an irate reply, 'Green?')

Over the years – especially those following the end of the war – there were luxuries and goods obtainable on board the liner or in the States, which were either unobtainable, scarce or far more expensive in the United Kingdom.

Tinned peaches were a luxury in the early days that could be taken ashore when going on leave as a treat for the family; Merchant Navy coupons were also available during the long period of post-war rationing, that enabled a crewman to buy extra warm clothing.

But some were never happy with the basic allowances and found that the only way to get extra cigarettes, nylons, ballpoint pens, etc, into Britain for their friends was to indulge in a little smuggling. Although a practice that could bring instant dismissal, many crew members could not resist the temptation but only a few would try to take it to the extreme.

With fashionable neckties in New York obtainable for $1 for 3; nylons at $6 per dozen pairs (which would sell for 3 guineas in the UK); US cigarettes at $1 per 200 carton which would sell for £1 in some Southampton pubs, the temptation often proved too great.

When the 'Rummage Squad', the Customs and Excise men, came on board with the pilot they would often search places like the Engine Room (the side plate of the steam condenser had to come off on one occasion with its hundreds of bolts having to be undone at first and then re-tightened) before the crew's accommodation was searched.

A couple of engineers wanted to get three thousand cigarettes ashore and decided to wait until they returned from two weeks' leave (as the *Queen Elizabeth* was laying up for her annual winter overhaul) before they took their 'booty' ashore.

Ninety-nine per cent of the time the liner's forward boiler rooms were used for maintaining in-port services, so the engineers concealed their packages in the after funnel casing.

Unfortunately for them a change in plans brought the after boilers into use, and by the time the two men returned from leave their contraband had been turned into dry brown tubes that crumbled to dust in their hands.

If, after the customs-men's search of the vessel, the crew's contraband was still intact, it had still to be taken through Dock Gate No. 4 where British Transport Police were on duty.

This proved to be less of a problem than it first seemed as a half-crown (12½p) coin concealed within the seaman's pass tendered for inspection ensured that his taxi would be waved through the gate. A lack of the two-and-sixpenny incentive would lead to the taxi and its passenger being thoroughly searched, thus taking up the valuable leave time of those in the taxis queuing behind.

The Southampton City Police got wind of the practice, raided the dock police office and temporarily took over the duties of search themselves. On the day this happened a long queue of taxis carrying crew members going on leave extended from the dock gate back to the ship.

As word of what was happening spread along the immobile rank whatever shipboard store the taxi's occupant might happen to have in his possession was quickly discarded.

Meat from the ship's cold store was a popular 'perk' and, as a result of the unexpected raid, dock workers arriving for work the morning after found the side of the road littered with hastily abandoned turkey legs and hams that were eagerly gathered up.

Anecdotes about the two great *Queen* liners abound and reflect a way of life that has now disappeared. These few recollections of some of the crew (which does not necessarily mean that all of them indulged in such 'lively' activities – many of them led a more peaceful life punctuated by seeing their families once a fortnight) will hopefully, balance other books which, however excellent, have tended to dwell on the more glamorous shipboard jobs or on stories about the famous passengers – part of the 'cargo' – whom the ship carried.

Although, as previously mentioned, the *Queen Elizabeth* did not enjoy the same affection that the Cunard men held for the *Queen Mary*, being described as the 'colder' of the two ships, she was nonetheless a popular ship. The loyalty that she was given by her crew, the lifeblood of any ship, was reflected in the service given to her passengers who patronised the ship in vast numbers time and time again.

In turn the numbers of passengers carried meant enormous profits for the proud steamship company which owned them and the two liners would repay their original investments many times over.

The two *Queen*'s became an establishment, a familiar sight to those who saw them sailing and arriving at their ports of call, a way of life to the crew who sailed them and source of an almost endless supply of increasing profits in the late 1950s to the Cunard Line.

It was a way of life that seemingly had no end and it was this complacency that would be destroyed completely within the next decade.

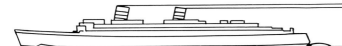

Chapter Eleven
"In Luck's Way"

The 'Cargo' – the passengers – varied greatly in both status and circumstance. From millionaires to politicians; from film stars to stars of industry; from tourists to students and from emigrants to the occasional stowaway, all wanted a fast or glamorous (or both) ride across the ocean.

Many passengers were loyal to the *Queen* for many years, others might wish to be seen travelling on the biggest ship afloat but the majority wanted a quick and, if they could afford it, comfortable passage to America, France or England.

Some had a long-held desire to travel on 'the' ship of their dreams and foremost amongst these was Her Majesty Queen Elizabeth (later to become the Queen Mother) who had expressed a wish that one day she might sail on the ship she had launched.

Before that day came, however, the Queen would visit the liner with her husband, King George VI. The King had missed the vessel's launch because of the crisis in Europe back in 1938.

On the fine summer's day of July 28th 1948, the Monarch and his consort, accompanied by their younger daughter Princess Margaret Rose, were received on board the flagship of Great Britain's merchant fleet.

The purpose of the royal visit was to enable Her Majesty to present the ship with her personal standard, framed and hung in the Main Restaurant. But the prime reason for the day's visit was for the Queen to unveil a portrait of herself.

Originally vetoing the idea of allowing her portrait to be hung in the ship when the liner was launched, the Queen had now relented and had consented to a painting being commissioned.

The portrait of Queen Elizabeth by Sir Oswald Birley that came to be hung in the Main Lounge.
The University Archives, the University of Liverpool

She had been persuaded to change her mind by her brother, the Hon. David Bowes-Lyon, recently appointed to the Board of the Cunard.

David Bowes-Lyon had previously been shown over the *Elizabeth* by her captain, Commodore Robert Thelwell. During an exchange of views about the various works of art and decor that they saw the captain said: 'You know, of course, that the *Queen Mary* has the big bronze medallion of the Queen Mother' (as Queen Mary was at that time) 'and in a glass case on the main staircase there is her own personal standard? In this ship we have no memento at all.'

David Bowes-Lyon took the hint, had a word with his sister and Sir Oswald Birley was given the commission to paint the portrait that now hung in the First Class Lounge.

To make room for it the large marquetry panel depicting 'The Canterbury Tales' (which had attracted so much acclaim when it first appeared) was re-hung at the head of the Main Hall stairway.

The Queen's '... cherished wish' that she might someday sail on the liner, materialised in October 1954 when, by now Queen Mother since the King's death, she embarked at the beginning of a tour of the United States and Canada.

Arriving on board on the eve of sailing, the Queen Mother's family accompanied and dined with her before making their farewells.

One of the unofficial strikes which plagued the '50s was in progress at that time, so the liner had been backed into the Ocean Dock, stem pointing towards the dock entrance, to enable her to achieve an easy departure should the strikers attempt to disrupt the sailing.

But the liner and her very special passenger had the full co-operation of the tugmen, and she sailed on time

A gala day for the great Cunarder occurred on 28th July 1948 when their Majesties King George V and Queen Elizabeth visited the liner. *Southampton City Museums*

with Commodore Sir Ivan Thompson in command. It was October 21st, yet another Trafalgar Day.

During the crossing the liner encountered rough weather but this did not deter the Queen from making daily tours to various parts of the ship, attending Divine Service on the Sunday and dining either in the Main Restaurant or in the Verandah Grill, the latter restaurant being so exclusive that in normal voyaging the First Class passengers lucky enough to obtain a seat there had to pay a supplement of 3 guineas – £3.15.

En passage to New York the *Queen Elizabeth* passed the east-bound *Queen Mary*. The great excitement that preceded the meeting grew to a crescendo, especially on the *Mary* whose passengers lined her rails watching the other liner with HM's standard fluttering at her masthead. As the two sisters sped towards the mid-ocean encounter, the *Mary*'s passengers first cheered the *Elizabeth* with her royal passenger as they passed and then watched the *Elizabeth* disappear astern as the gap between the two *Queens* of the Atlantic rapidly widened at 70 mph.

The Queen Mother replied to a signal from the *Queen Mary* on which she would be returning to England at the end of her tour:

'I send you my greetings and good wishes to all on board. I hope you get better weather soon.

Elizabeth R.'

In 1953 the two liners transported guests and spectators alike to and from England for the great event of the year, the Coronation of Queen Elizabeth II.

Various celebrations were held on board the *QE* as a salute to the grand occasion, and a special menu was devised that would reflect the royal event. Presented on Monday, June 1st, the dishes had been suitably dubbed with such regal annotations as 'Smoked Salmon Britannia', 'Fillet of Lemon Sole Buckingham', 'Guinea Chicken Clarence House' and 'Sirloin Steak la Reine'.

Coronation Day itself found the *Lizzie* away from the shores of a very Merrie England and docking alongside Pier 90 in New York. But, on the following day, recalled bedroom steward Terry Little, a film of the pageantry and crowning was flown over to the States and shown in another favourite haunt of Cunard men – 'Maxi's San Susie' bar.

Commodore Harry Grattidge also recalled an anecdote that arose a short while after the event, in his book, 'Captain of the *Queens*'.

The Commodore had been present at the Coronation in Westminster Abbey as one of three representatives of the Merchant Service. A month after the crowning he was back on board. The Marquess of Salisbury was travelling and was one of his table guests.

One evening the film 'A Queen is Crowned' was being shown in the ship's cinema and the Marquess, a quiet person who apparently preferred listening rather than talking, asked the Commodore to accompany him to see the film. His main aim was to see how he looked during the ceremony as, in his capacity as Lord President of the Council, he had taken an active part in the noble pageant.

When the two men arrived in the packed cinema the film had already begun so, in the semi-darkness that pervades all cinemas, they edged their way into two seats in the back row.

Commodore Grattidge continued: 'Before long a stifled chuckling became audible. One or two people turned round. All was quiet for a moment or two, then a sudden gurgle. Someone 'shushed' indignantly. This time the gurgling stopped for good, but from time to time there came from the darkness the stifled sounds of a man who knows he must control his mirth whatever the cost. It was Lord Salisbury, overcome by the anguish of his own face as he wrestled with the enormous weight of the Sword of State!'

Amongst many loyal devotees of the two *Queens* were the Duke and Duchess of Windsor. (Their allegiance was later transferred to the American, record-breaking, super-liner *United States* when she appeared on the Atlantic in July 1956, easily grabbing the Blue Riband from the *Queen Mary* with a speed of 35 knots).

The Duchess was for ever sparklingly gregarious but her husband's moods could vary. Sometimes he was delightfully animated and then his mood could sway in the other direction when he appeared to be inwardly reflecting on what might have been.

One Christmas Eve the Duke descended to the 'Pig and Whistle' where a crew's concert was about to commence. He was greeted with cries of 'Good old Teddy!' and' God Bless the Prince of Wales!' Changing his mind after first asking to play the drums, the Duke decided to address the crew from the makeshift stage, beginning with 'My fellow Englishmen ....' At the finish he sat down with Chief Officer (later Commodore) Donald MacLean and Lord Sefton in a space on a bench made by two burly, dungareed and singleted stokers shifting their positions. The Duke then proffered Royal cigars to those around him. He thoroughly enjoyed the ensuing show – probably of a standard as risque as ever. (Whether or not the famous 'Jane' sang that night is not recorded!)

The start of that particular crossing found the Duke almost escorted off the Bridge as a trespasser on the 'Holy of Holies.' It was not until the Chief Officer (sent by the captain, who had as yet not recognised the interloper's identity, to perform the act of eviction) approached the Duke that he realised who he was. After a few remarks about the weather and a request to be able to stay on the Bridge, the Duke of Windsor was discreetly left alone with his own thoughts, watching the lights of Cherbourg (where he had boarded the liner by tender) recede into the darkening distance of a bitter, sleet-filled night of 21st December 1949.

Many members of international royalty also chose the *Queen Elizabeth* as their means of transport to and from the States.

Ex-King Michael of Rumania, and his mother Queen Helen; Crown Prince Akhito of Japan; Maharajahs with gold buttons studded with diamonds and their fabulously be-jewelled consorts – all preferred the luxury they found on board.

The Sheik of Kuwait travelled with a case containing several gross of gold watches which he liked to give away to those who served him well. Young 17 year old Prince Mohammed Feisal (later crowned King Feisal II of Iran) forgot his camera just before disembarking at Southampton in November 1952. Although he was supposed to have been the first passenger ashore he returned to look for his mislaid property. The ship was dressed overall for the arrival and a regimental band waited for him to disembark.

The band had been instructed to strike up when they saw the first passenger – presumed to be the Prince – appear. It was never ascertained who was the more surprised – the performing bandsmen or the first man actually ashore, none other than Charlie Chaplin!

British Labour politicians including Messrs. Morrison, Bevan and Brown crossed on the *QE* (important Socialists seemed to revel in the luxurious living that the Cunard Company provided, noted Commodore Robert Thelwell) as well as prominent Conservatives such as Sir Anthony Eden, 'Rab' Butler and their wives (Mrs Butler was always knitting, Commodore Grattidge later recalled), Edward Heath and many other figures of politics whether British or Foreign, Left or Right, Communist, Royalist, totalitarian or democrat – all seemed to be 'levelled' by the superb conditions that they found on board.

The Russian diplomat Molotov travelled on the *Queen Elizabeth* on several occasions but his famous – or rather infamous – 'Niets' in the United Nations seemed to mellow into 'Da's' whilst on board. An interpreter travelled with his entourage although he could speak very passable English.

However, Commodore Thelwell seemed to be unaware of this fact, as the feared diplomat had only spoken to him in Russian translated through his interpreter. So when the Commodore arrived at Molotov's suite after accepting an invitation to cocktails, the Russian smilingly greeted him in perfect English. When a surprised and momentarily undiplomatic captain retorted: 'Ah! so you can speak English Mr Molotov!', the smile disappeared from the face of a now wary Russian, and the captain was thankful when he was later called away from the party.

In September 1960, Tito, the late President of Yugoslavia, boarded the liner, which respectfully flew his personal standard at the main-masthead, at Cherbourg where he had arrived in his armoured train. The security surrounding his crossing to a Security Council meeting of the UN infused the trip with a military atmosphere not experienced since the war. Randolph Churchill was also on the ship for that voyage, his earlier chagrin aroused during the *Queen*'s grounding in 1946 apparently having long disappeared.

But not all the *Queen Elizabeth*'s passengers were so seriously minded.

Many of the stars of the world of entertainment performed during a voyage, and their audiences of fellow passengers were encouraged to make a collection – customarily for seamen's charities.

Sophie Tucker, that bubbling mountain of personality and fun, gave a non-stop, three hour performance of songs and monologues during a crossing in 1961. Her audience was left clamouring for more.

In November 1949 Kathleen Ferrier, a singer of a completely different genre, left her audience spellbound by the ethereal quality of her exceptionally beautiful voice. She was followed by Field Marshal Lord Montgomery who gave a short speech in favour of the seamen's charities for which the evening was as usual being held. The proceeds from that evening represented a record to date – £400 collected in an enthusiastic ten minutes!

Actor Phil Silvers – forever remembered for his television role as the scheming, fast talking 'Sergeant Bilko' – gave a performance one evening that equalled the talents of his television character. Asked to perform the duties of auctioneer (selling sweepstake tickets for the time of arrival), he brought Sergeant Bilko's skills of painlessly extracting money from his 'customers' into use. He gradually coaxed up the bids for the favourite ticket through a crescendo of humorous banter, until only two contenders were left in the bidding – Lady Docker and a Texan oilman. When the offers reached £100 Lady Docker decided to turn the bidding to guineas (21/- or £1.05). 'Guineas?' Bilko asked with serious incredulity as his grasp of the financial situation momentarily wavered, 'What kind of money is THAT?'

Phil Silvers was equally at home in the company of the crew. Of Silvers' invitation to the Engineers' Ward Room, engineer Lovell Taylor wrote:

'What a great character old Phil is. He's got this crowd of us round him, including the Chief Engineer, up in the wardroom. He's performing the three-card trick "Find the Lady" for the completely baffled .... Chief Engineer. He just can't pick out the 'queen' card and, what with Phil's

A sparkling *Queen* on a sparkling sea.   *The University Archives, the University of Liverpool*

slick line of patter, he gets more embarrassed by the minute.

'If the Chief Engineer can't do a simple thing like "Finding the Lady" how do you ever manage to run a ship like this?' he says, 'thats what I'd like to know, how can a dumb guy like you ever run this goddam ship?'

'We all fall about laughing, and the Chief made some lame excuse to get the .... out of there.'

Other personalities were less gregarious. The famed American conductor Stokowski (well-known for conducting the music in Walt Disney's film 'Fantasia') travelled, incognito under his Polish Christian forenames in their anglicised form of 'Antony Stanley,' with his young wife to whom he was most attentive – almost to the point of resenting any steward or bell boy who held her chair or opened a door for her before he had a chance to do so.

Rita Hayworth and Rosalind Russell had also travelled under assumed names when they travelled.

Boarding the liner in New York Charlie Chaplin set out on the start of what was to be a nostalgic visit to his birth place in the East End of London.

Almost half-way across the Atlantic the famed clown received a message from the United States, telling him that his long-standing permit enabling him to live and work in that country had been rescinded.

The anti-American activities committee which had been investigating his (and thousands of other Americans') communist leanings had found that, many years previously, he had donated $100 to the now outlawed party at a time when it was seen to be the only apparent champion against oppression. This small gesture was considered enough to banish him to an enforced exile in Switzerland. (At the time, Cunard crew members were also asked by the immigration authorities, on each arrival in New York, if they had any communistic tendencies or sympathies. 'I'm a commis' the young waiters would reply, tongue-in-cheek, to questions as to what they were!)

Earl Mountbatten of Burma, always bronzed and fit in spite of the vast amount of work with which he travelled, enjoyed the hospitality of the liner, and Lord Montgomery of Alamein enjoyed a 63rd birthday party given in his honour. Sir Adrian Boult, that most gentle of English orchestral conductors (on board the *Mary* he had conducted the occupants of the Main Restaurant in singing 'Happy Birthday' to Captain Donald Sorrell), travelled as did playwrights Noel Coward and Tennessee Williams.

Sportsmen carried over the years included such boxing champions as Joe Louis, Randolph Turpin and Sugar Ray Robinson.

Organised groups journeyed on the liner and sometimes entertained the passengers; the renowned Vienna Boys Choir sang in the Main Lounge to great acclaim.

Amongst the more unusual passengers was counted one Edgar Foster who booked a return passage in July 1953. Fifty four years of age and a clothing businessman from Birmingham, he had an almost unique hobby – diving from unusual platforms. Was it to celebrate the Coronation that he paid £500 for his round trip in the *Queen Elizabeth* to pursue his self-taught pursuit? Once in New York he balanced on the ship's rail and, to the cheers of his accomplice who had held his legs as he precariously balanced above the murky waters into which he would soon be plummeting, he made his self-gratifying plunge.

He also wanted to dive from the *Lizzie*'s Bridge on the liner's return to Southampton, but a shoulder hurt during his dive into the Hudson – and the captain's downright refusal to give him permission – dissuaded him from his ambition. At the end of his voyage he still felt that his fare had been money well-spent!

At the other end of the passenger strata David Stroyman of Brooklyn, Massachusetts, must have – in February 1956 and at 71 years of age – ranked as the oldest stowaway ever to attempt a free passage on the liner.

Hoping to catch some of the *Queen*'s glamour on film the Rank Organisation based a movie musical 'As Long as They're Happy' around the liner in 1954, and in the 1960s two television documentaries were made on board.

The first was produced by the now defunct Southern Television company of Southampton, and was called 'Profile of a Commodore', the position held at that time by Donald MacLean. The documentary was broadcast on Thursday, 9th November 1961.

Another Commodore, Harry Grattidge, had earlier become involved in film making but in an advisory role only, when he became Technical Advisor to the Rank Organisation when the classic *Titanic* film 'A Night To Remember' was made in 1958.

An American television company made the second documentary which revolved around the lives of the captain, chief engineer and chief steward during one voyage.

The *Lizzie* returned to the big screen in 1959, appearing briefly in Columbia's 'The Mouse That Roared'. During the film she was attacked with arrows (sticking into the Bridge above the head of the captain) fired by Peter Sellers and his bunch of chain-mailed soldiers crossing the Atlantic on board the tug tender *Paladin*, *en route* to attack the United States.

Towards the end of the decade that followed, the *Queen Elizabeth* would make a last appearance in one of the exciting series of 'James Bond' movies, 'The Man With the Golden Gun'.

Throughout her career the *Queen* was commanded by men who had reached the pinnacle of their profession. The officers under their command were also highly qualified, with Masters' and Extra-Masters' certificates, but all this skill was needed to navigate the world's largest liner over the world's (at times) roughest ocean.

The North Atlantic Ocean would on occasion delay the *Queen Elizabeth*, sometimes by many hours, through storm, fog, ice and, even in late post-war years, by a drifting mine spotted in the English Channel!

A severe storm could cause damage to both ship and those on board as well as to the timetable. In the latter event some of the lost time could be made up on an eastward crossing by a quick dash across the English Channel between Cherbourg and Southampton – or rather the Nab Tower.

The *Queen* often broke her own records for this short passage making one particularly fast crossing in March 1958, when a time of 2 hours 24 minutes was recorded.

A storm in December 1959 delayed the *QE*'s arrival in Southampton (under the command of George Morris) by 37 hours. A 75 mph gale, during which waves of 50 to 60 feet in height were observed, had been encountered.

During the gale a porthole had been blown in on 'A' deck, flooding a cabin – A94 – and injuring its occupant. Two thousand pieces of crockery and glassware were also broken during the storm.

Amongst those on board were J.D. Goulandris, the Greek shipping magnate, and the British film actress, Margaret Leighton.

On disembarking Miss Leighton told the Southampton Southern Evening Echo:

'It was horrible, but I was terribly impressed with the way the ship rode the storm. It was much more comfortable than I have experienced in other ships in rough weather.'

After a similar gale – but with reputedly even larger waves – earlier in February 1957 (and with Jack Buchanan the film actor on board), the ship apparently '.... rode beautifully because of the stabilisers.'

In the seven years following the entry of both *Queens* entry into post-war service it was found that many passengers – especially women – were terrified of the rough conditions of which the North Atlantic was capable in wintertime.

Convinced that the delays, changes, bumpy and cramped dash offered by pre-jet aircraft was preferable to the 'horrors' of winter sea travel, these 'lost' passengers had to be attracted back to the sea.

Deciding to compete against the wings in the sky, Cunard put plans into action to equip their ships with wings under the ocean by fitting the two mighty *Queens* with Denny-Brown stabilisers.

This equipment had previously been successfully fitted to the much smaller Cunarders *Media* and *Parthia* and it was now time to start the huge conversion jobs on the *Queens* intended, as the publicists said, 'to smooth your way across the Atlantic'. Work started on preparing the *Elizabeth* whilst she was still at sea – fifteen months before the actual fitting of the stabilisers was due to take place.

During this preparation work oil tanks were converted to become stabiliser machinery compartments. Existing machinery was also resited, not an easy task since the liner's designers had used the available space to full advantage.

The fitting of the stabilisers took place during the *Queen Elizabeth*'s 1955 long winter overhaul which began with her dry docking on January 21st, bumping both sides of the dock as she entered it.

Two sets of stabilisers were fitted to the *Queen* with a distance of 150 feet between sets. Originally it had been hoped that one set of larger fins would be sufficient, but the small space available between hull and dock walls precluded this.

John I. Thornycroft, the Southampton firm of shipbuilders and shipfitters, had made full size mock-ups of the equipment to ensure that any foreseeable problems could be overcome well before the work was done. They certainly had a difficult job especially in reorganising the internal layout of the ship in the way of the stabiliser machinery.

The dry dock also only had cranes along one of its walls so the ship's own equipment had to be used in conjunction with the dock facilities to cajole the new equipment from one side of the dock to the other.

The installation work required 5 miles of cable, 12,000

feet of piping, 600 feet of trunking and 4 motors of 80 horsepower each.

Each stabiliser fin had an outreach of 12 feet 6 inches and a width of 7 feet 3 inches. Both sets could be extended and operated independently of the other so that only one set need be operated in a moderate swell.

Operated from the bridge the forward set had a righting moment of 11,500 ton/ft and the after set exerted 14,000 ton/ft. It was calculated that a roll could be reduced by 75% within a very short time.

The *Queen* came out of her longer than usual refit of ten weeks on 23rd March, having spent some time alongside a 'wet' berth after leaving dry dock. The first priority was to test the new installations and this was scheduled for the following weekend.

The trials took the form of a short cruise to the Lizard with several guests boarding the liner on the eve of departure.

Unknown to those peacefully sleeping in their beds that night, an emergency arose in the Engine Room which the engineers struggled to overcome before the rest of the ship awoke.

At 4 am a fuel pump had jammed and the ship suffered a severe loss of power. This resulted in the boilers going out, the level of water in the boilers going down and a loss of steam. All electricity supplies had to be cut to conserve what little steam there was until the jammed fuel pumps could be induced to work, thus gradually bringing back into operation all the vital machinery that had been brought to a halt.

When underway at last, only a moderate swell was encountered so an artificially induced roll was created by operating the stabilisers in reverse, achieved by reversing the response of the gyro control.

Once the liner had developed a roll of sufficient dimension, the gyro control – and hence the stabilisers – were 'normalised' to reduce the motion, which they did quite satisfactorily.

On the first post-refit voyage to New York the stabilisers' designer, Sir William Wallace, travelled with the ship. He later declared himself to be ' .... very satisfied' with the equipment especially as the ship had encountered winds during her eastward run of around 50 miles per hour for a forty-eight hour period. The *Lizzie*'s captain, Commodore Sir Ivan Thompson said that his ship was ' ... as steady as a rock' during the rough weather.

As mentioned earlier the two *Queens* each had two annual overhauls. The summer overhaul was a short one of about one week's duration generally during late July, early August. This consisted of a general smartening up with a coat of paint and carrying out small repairs and maintenance in readiness for the peak, lucrative summer season.

The second – and main – overhaul lasted from five to six weeks during the off-peak winter period and could occur anywhere between late November and early March.

It was during the winter lay-up that a great deal of essential maintenance, survey and testing was done on the liner's hull, machinery, fittings and furnishings in order to keep the ship at the top of the league.

In 1956 the *Queen* appeared from her winter overhaul fitted with 'wings under the water' which helped Cunard promote their 'Smooth Your Way Across the Atlantic' campaign in an endeavour to attract passengers back to winter crossings.
Southern Newspapers plc,
Southampton

The liner spent about three weeks in the King George V dry dock at Southampton, with the remainder of the period being spent alongside a quay on a wet berth. Up to fifteen hundred men swarmed over the ship, untidying what had hitherto been immaculate.

The amount of work to be done was prodigious.

As the water in the dock was pumped out so workmen in punts – attached to the liner by 'wash-lines' – ranged to and fro along the length of the liner as she sat on the dock blocks scrubbing the underwater hull clear of weed and barnacles as the water level fell.

When at last the dock was dry and the liner snug on the blocks, the three sixteen-ton anchors and 330 fathoms of cable were lowered to the dock bottom. Each anchor was then surveyed, cleaned and painted as was every 2 cwt (51 kg) link of the cables that snaked across the dock beneath the sharp, yacht-like bow that towered above.

At each winter overhaul one of the four propeller tail shafts, each weighing 37 tons, would be extracted and surveyed as would the propellers or their bosses (cones).

During the January 1961 winter overhaul a new propeller was fitted to the inner port shaft. Much lighter than the one it replaced, the new propeller was made of a nickel bronze alloy instead of manganese bronze. It proved to be effective at higher speeds (the shaft turning at a few revolutions less as a consequence) but tended to 'shunt' its propeller shaft at lower speeds, with a knocking noise coming from the plummer blocks.

The small door in the rudder was also opened and men would enter its interior to inspect and paint. Once the access panel was re-bolted into position the watertightness of the rudder would be tested with compressed air.

Inlets and outlets, normally underwater, were inspected and the 15,000 square yards of underwater hull was then painted with seven tons of primer and anti-fouling compositions applied by 120 painters. Another large quantity of paint would be used to freshen up those marvellous funnels, the buff masts, the white superstructure and black hull.

While the *Elizabeth* was in dry-dock only one of her boilers was kept fired in order to maintain essential ship services. Fresh water and electricity were supplied, meanwhile, via connections made to the dockside.

Concurrent with the work being carried out on the exterior of the ship, the machinery had also to be inspected and tested. 160,000 boiler tubes (some of which – the upper economiser or pre-heat tubes – were replaced by glass versions in the 1962 refit. This was because the steel variants had to be previously replaced almost yearly due to

disintegration caused by the gases – having reached a low temperature and 'dew point' – releasing sulphuric acid in the tubes which caused them almost to crumble to the touch) were tested and hundreds of feet of oil pipeline carefully checked.

257,000 turbine blades, 30 oil and water tanks, 35 lifts, 30,000 lightbulbs, 750 electric clocks, 600 telephones, 530 electric motors (ranging from 0.25 to 300 horsepower) – all had to be checked, tested, and replaced where necessary, painted where needed, along with a thousand other jobs that had to be done.

The hotel services were also busy during the lay-up stocktaking their hardware and linen.

A lot of logoed Company tableware usually disappeared during the course of each year through the eagerness of souvenir hunters, and the chief stewards had a good deal to account for on their inventories: 54,000 pieces of china and earthenware (including 21,000 plates, 8,500 cups, 7,000 saucers) plus 26,000 pieces of glassware, and 40,000 pieces of silver plate consisting of 10,500 knives, 10,000 forks and 6,750 spoons.

Three and a half thousand items of furniture and equipment were taken ashore for survey, whilst painters and polishers smartened up metalwork and the huge areas of rare veneers.

When the winter lay-up was finally complete a mess usually remained in the crews' 'Working Alley' but, within a day of leaving refit, all had been tidied and cleaned.

Once more the *Queen Elizabeth* was ready to take on what both the North Atlantic and the contemporary, ultra-discerning, travelling public would demand of her.

Sometimes more would be asked of the ship than

A stern view of the *Lizzie* in the King George V dry dock in Southampton during an annual overhaul.　　　　　*Author's collection*

would normally be expected but she and her equipment had been designed to withstand almost everything that would come her way.

As has already been noted fog was often one of her greatest adversaries either delaying the liner or putting her into danger.

It was in such thick weather that the *Queen* was approaching Cherbourg, eastbound, in January 1965.

The liner's last incident at the port had occurred in November 1953, when she had sustained a 20 foot buckle in her side plates after bumping into the pier. Her sister had been less fortunate – almost disastrously so – and had gone aground on the Seleine Bank within the harbour confines. Only by sheer luck had she grounded on one of

Before the construction of Southampton's Ocean Terminal building the gangways were lifted between quayside and ship by crane. *The University Archives, the University of Liverpool*

the strongest parts of her hull – otherwise she would have surely broken her back.

But now, on 25th January, the *Queen Elizabeth* under the command of Commodore Frederick Watts – and with pilot Captain Marcel Castel on board – was brought to a halt as the liner approached Cherbourg. Visibility in the thick fog that prevailed ranged from a mile down to zero.

It was low water and the *Queen* started to drift sideways in the oily water, an unnoticed drift that was brought gently to a halt as the liner grounded on a mudbank.

She was there for an anxious half-hour but, as the tide rose, she floated easily off the underwater mound.

She had grounded on her portside fore-end and, on docking in Cherbourg, divers were sent down to inspect her hull. Nothing untoward was found and a similar inspection on her arrival in Southampton also revealed nothing.

Fog had proved to be more troublesome six years earlier on the Stateside of 'The Pond'.

Visibility was down to less than two hundred feet as, on 29th July 1959, the *Queen* left New York.

Her pilot was manually sounding the ship's siren to warn other ships which might be in her vicinity and this intermittent distinctive booming was heard and recognised

by the officers of the United States Line's cargo vessel *American Hunter*.

On the Cunarder engines were stopped and two radar screens (2 mile and 4 mile ranges) were manned. There were several 'targets' on each and, as one target appeared to be closing, the *QE*'s engines were put into reverse.

But it was too late. The 'target', the *American Hunter* (also with engines put astern), found the giant liner crossing her bow, the latter still having a forward motion.

A collision was unavoidable. The cargo ship hit the liner inflicting dents in some plates and a hole below the starboard hawse pipe, (later temporarily repaired with cement on a quick return to New York). The American ship merely suffered a two foot dent.

The *Elizabeth* arrived in Southampton only 24 hours behind schedule.

Five years later the *Queen* had another brush with yet another GI.

She was moored alongside her quay in Southampton when the *General S.B. Buckner* arrived in port on 16th September 1964. Caught by the strong wind, the American ship, still slowly underway, was blown over to the *Queen*'s berth and brushed against the *Elizabeth*'s side. There was no structural damage.

January 1959 saw the *Queen* fogbound on the last leg of an eastward trip. For fifty hours she was delayed – firstly just south of the Nab Tower and then for a long period in Cowes Roads. Her passengers were taken off by the tenders *Paladin*, *Romsey* and *Vecta*.

Fog, collision, storm and grounding are but four of the many hazards that can be encountered at sea but perhaps the most feared is fire.

It had been fire that had caused the premature demise of the fabled *Normandie* and many other fine ships, and so the men of the *Queen Elizabeth* were ever vigilant in protecting their beautiful ship from a similar fate.

However, the *Queen* – like any large town – experienced several fires during her term as Empress of the Atlantic, usually of a minor and easily controllable nature.

What with carbon dioxide blanketing for the holds, baggage rooms etc; pressurised water sprinklers in accommodation and public rooms and a full-time, manned fire station, the *Queen* was as well-protected against fire as she could be under current legislation.

Small fires would break out now and then. For example, the Engine Room fought fires which perhaps started in the pipe lagging, impregnated with the fine oily mist pervading that particular area.

But on three occasions the blazes that arose on board could have had consequences of great magnitude.

The first, as the *Elizabeth* was being converted to her peace time role in 1946, has already been recounted. The second occurred whilst the liner was in dry-dock during her winter overhaul of January 1953.

This fire started at around 8.15 pm in the wardrobe of cabin M93 which, as a result, was badly damaged. Charred remains were taken away for expert investigation but the cause of the fire remained a mystery.

The day after the M93 fire – only a few hours later – the Southampton Fire Brigade was called out for a second

An impressive view of the *Queen Elizabeth* in drydock at Southampton. Spare propellers were usually kept on the dockside by the pumping station at the right-hand side of the dock gate. *Southern Newspapers plc, Southampton*

time, this time to extinguish a small blaze in a pile of oily rags found in cabin C146.

And for a third time within forty eight hours the Brigade rushed to the ship, this time to find that the alarm had been false.

With the industrial unrest and the very militant 'unionists' who were active in the country at that time, it is still surprising that the first of the fires remains a mystery in view of the subsequent alarms.

Seven years later, in September 1960, a serious fire broke out in the main electrical switchboard (during a westbound voyage in the English Channel) which took a hundred men of the ship's crew three hours to control. Several cabins had to be rebuilt as a result and thirty starboard cabins on three First Class decks remained untenable for the next trip.

Danger in entering and leaving port was ever present and the nearest that the *Queen Elizabeth* came to complete and instantaneous destruction was only narrowly avoided. She had just left Southampton and Commodore Thelwell recalled the event in his book 'I Captained the Big Ships':

'Ten-forty. A tongue of orange flame shot as usual from the high chimney of the Fawley Refinery. The scene was familiar, comforting.

'But as we approached the jetty, a not-so-familiar sight swung into view. Holt [the pilot] and I saw it at the same time.

"My God!" I said, involuntarily.

'Near the jetty a black blob of a tanker lay at anchor, almost athwart the channel and heading westerly into the path of the *Queen Elizabeth*. Further south, a second tanker was attempting to make fast to buoys and sheering easterly in the process.

'Holt snapped out an order at once: "Reduce speed". He waited for a moment until the order was transmitted. "They told me before we sailed that the tankers would be safely berthed and out of our path", said Holt in his quiet voice.

'Those who have served under me in the big ships will concede, I think, that whatever my defects, a tendency to panic is not one: but I confess that at that moment I was near to panic. Pilot Holt was navigating the ship but the responsibility for the safety of the lives of the passengers and crew, and for the safety of the ship itself, was mine alone.

'And I knew, as Holt did, that we were heading for certain disaster with hardly any cards in our hands to play and little to do except wait and pray that our luck would hold.

'For the tankers were loaded with oil. The slightest collision would generate sparks and the tankers would become more lethal than a torpedo discharged into the unprotected belly of the ship I commanded.

' ... I began to think of the orders I would give when the searing explosion took place – assuming that I was still alive to give orders and that there were any officers and seamen left to carry them out. My war experience had not, fortunately, included the sight of a tanker attacked by enemy aircraft, but friends had told me how terrible it could be and I had a picture in my mind of broken bodies, a smashed ship and a sea of blazing oil. It was quite possible that the explosion would be so violent that my gigantic ship would be sent to the bottom of Southampton Water before we could lower any of the boats.

'Whilst these fearful thoughts raced through my mind, I glanced away from the tanker for a few moments. The white, tense faces of the staff captain and chief officer showed that they had seen what the pilot and I had seen. Below us on the decks the passengers strolled about in the sunlight or leaned over the starboard side to gaze in awe at the refinery. The ship was gliding to almost certain destruction yet only a handful of us, of all the souls on board, knew it.

'A quiet voice interrupted my thoughts. 'You know, Captain,' said Pilot Holt, 'this is the sort of situation that can cause a considerable amount of danger.'

'I could not and cannot recall ever hearing such an understatement in my lifetime.

'We both now stared ahead, unable to take our eyes away from the two tankers as we bore down on them.

'Reduce speed – dead slow.'

'I knew as well as Pilot Holt that we dared not reduce speed any more or the rudder would be useless and the ship hopelessly out of control. We had gone to the limit of what we could do in the matter of speed.

'Ease the helm.'

'Only superb steering and luck – especially luck – could now save the ship.

'Port easy. Port more.'

'We had sailed at high water, and the tide was behind us and a still freshening wind would have made it hard to keep the ship on course at the best of times, without additional hazard. Yet Pilot Holt's modulated voice contained no hint of nervousness.

'A hundred yards and we should know our fate.

'Fifty yards.

'Now we were within twenty yards of the leading tanker and we could see her cable across the bow and apparently leading somewhere astern. The two tugs which had been berthing her stood off. The wind blew harder and, in spite of all the pilot could do, caused the ship to drift nearer the tanker.

'Fifteen yards to go – fifteen agonizing yards which could just as well end in death as in life. I could scarcely breathe as the gap between the tanker and the track we were taking narrowed inexorably.

'Ten yards. The crisis was on us and over almost at the same time. The *Queen* was holding to her course.

'I think we're in luck's way this morning, said the quiet voice of Pilot Holt.

'A few more moments and we were safe, though with no more than ten feet to spare. The passengers on the rails, cheering and waving to the tanker's frightened crew, would never know why there was not a wave in return or how close they had been to a terrible death.'

The second tanker was passed by with five hundred feet between the two ships.

The *Queen* sailed on, but the next few years would see a certain change in her fortunes.

Chapter Twelve
'Lovely to the Last ...'
(Byron)

The years spanning 1947 and 1956 were hugely profitable for Cunard with their ships sometimes carrying 50% of the total North Atlantic traffic. In one year alone this meant a million people travelling by Cunard, representing a record for any company.

The two *Queens* recovered their original building costs by many score and, because of the phenomenal success of their ships, the board of Cunard became complacent about the competition of the propeller-driven aircraft which was never considered a real threat: people would always prefer to cross the ocean by liner and preferably by Cunard!

With the advent of the high-flying jet aircraft, however, all this suddenly and dramatically changed. 1957 proved to be the irreversible turning point when an equal number of people were transported by jet as were carried by ship.

After that fateful year there was a steady change of balance in favour of the jets: thereafter the fortunes of the North Atlantic shipping companies began to change, all experiencing an accelerating decline into the abyss of

oblivion. Instead of the scores of passenger liners operated by dozens of international companies there is now, in the late '80s only one true transatlantic liner left: one that belongs to the first company to start a regular fleet service across the Atlantic in 1840 – the Cunard: sadly, the ship – *Queen Elizabeth 2* – operates the route only in the summer months.

The decline that was yet to come was sensed by Cunard as early as 1957. Although after that date the revenue from the passenger side of the business would begin to fall, the cargo profits would remain buoyant for a while longer; that is, until the advent of container ships – the 'box boats' – each of which could carry the cargo equivalent of several conventional cargo ships but cheaply and more quickly.

But the passenger trade was affected adversely almost immediately and this decline was brought into highlight by the economic performances of the *Queen Mary* and *Queen Elizabeth*. On one eastward trip the number of stewards on

After yet another Atlantic crossing the *Queen Elizabeth* arrives in the Hudson River, giving her passengers the never-to-be-tired-of thrill of the Manhattan skyline.

Queen Elizabeth Historical Society

With her upper decks crowded with passengers enjoying the spectacle the *Queen Elizabeth* steams serenely through the Coronation Fleet Review of 1953.
Southern Newspapers plc, Southampton

board the *Lizzie* actually outnumbered their charges!

In spite of the recurrent losses the *Queen Elizabeth* could still carry, on occasion, an almost full complement. In June 1963, for example, over two thousand passengers were carried on one trip. Not bad for a 'dying' service!

In the 'sixties receipts for Cunard were in the region of £22m per year but the passenger carrying business continued to lose money – the £1.9m in 1962, £1.6m in 1964 and £3m in 1965 being the worst losses with lesser, but still severe, losses incurred in the years between.

Drastic surgery of both ships and men would be needed before the company could become, once again, a viable, commercial proposition.

It was not only the declining fortunes of the company's business that threatened the fleet of which the *Queen Elizabeth* was still the flagship. Labour disputes at sea and ashore also menaced, or promised to menace, the liner's scheduled services and on such occasions she was used as a massive pawn – a prime target – in various disputes involving tugmen, dockers (usually supplied by the local ship repairers), longshoremen (in New York) or the crew, either singularly or collectively. These men obviously felt that if they could interrupt either of the *Queens'* schedules then their case would be won.

In November 1948 an early success was scored by strikers. A longshoremen's strike was underway in New York and, as the liner was about to leave Southampton, the *Queen Elizabeth*'s crew 'came out' in sympathy as they regarded the ship's sailing as a 'strike-breaking' strategy.

There then followed a succession of events which continued even after the New York strike had ended. Tides were missed, delays were caused by fogs and a belated strike was called by the catering department.

Food supplies almost became a problem (the *Queen* normally stored in New York). Effluent discharged from the ship accumulated in the dock around her, causing worries about health.

1,000 of the 1,500 who remained of the original 2,200 passengers who had boarded the liner then added their own protests to those of the crew. After fourteen continuous days spent on board they protested that they could not afford to go ashore to stay in hotels etc and subsequently staged their own strike by refusing to leave the ship.

However, on 2nd December, and after sixteen days of strikes and latterly fog, the ship sailed on the same tide as the *Queen Mary* and *Aquitania*, a unique event in the peacetime history of all three vessels.

The mid '50s saw some unpleasant scenes as 'peaceful' pickets jostled passengers as well as crew, first at the dock gates and then at the quayside during an unofficial dispute.

In spite of the ugly scenes ashore, the *Queen* managed to sail: not to do so would be unthinkable and, besides, in sailing the strike could be broken.

As the *Elizabeth* pulled away from the Ocean Terminal jeers from the malcontents on the quayside were drowned by a few well-timed blasts on the ship's sirens.

It was felt by some of the long-serving and loyal members of the crew that much of the trouble on board had been caused by a particular young element of the crew. National Service was still in force and the young men of the country were given the choice of either joining one of the forces or serving in the Merchant Navy.

In the section that chose the latter alternative (the pay – plus any tips – provided an income many times that which a National Serviceman could expect), there were a few disruptive types, some of whom unfortunately had joined the Cunard. When dissatisfaction was expressed by the regular crew on matters of limited concern the young 'conscripts', lacking in long-term loyalty, would attempt – by fair means or foul – to exacerbate the situation, sometimes with dubious success.

But these disputes could often highlight the skill of the ship's navigators and engineers.

During strikes, either by dockers in Southampton, by longshoremen in New York or by tugmen, the *Queen* would have to be berthed unaided.

In 1957 the *Elizabeth* docked in her British port with tugs but with only half the usual number of stevedores in attendance; but the greatest feats of docking, unaided by striking tugs, took place in New York and earned the admiration of both mariners and the press.

Commodore Marr recalled the last time that the *Queen Elizabeth* was docked in such circumstances in his most readable autobiography 'The Queens and I'.

The idea was to wait for slack water – that short moment of still water between tides – in the River Hudson (problems were sometimes caused by 'freshlets' or Winter-melt water coming from up-country) and then to pivot the liner's bow either about a lowered anchor cable or about the 'knuckle' at the outer, near corner of the pier.

The ship would then be swung round until she was pointing towards the shore and laying parallel with the pier. The ship was then pulled in using her own hawsers previously taken ashore by row-boat.

Docking a giant ship in such circumstances always attracted a lot of press attention and, although practiced with great precision, was fraught with danger; often several dozen telegraph orders passed between Bridge and Engine Room during the execution of the delicate manoeuvre.

Of all the strikes and disputes that hit the *Elizabeth* the ultimately most catastrophic was the great Seamen's Strike of 1966. The strike brought Britain's merchant marine to a halt. However, great benefits were obtained for the seamen involved but these benefits would be of an unknowingly short term nature for many, as the British merchant navy would soon go into decline.

On 16 May 1966 the *QE* became one of the first major ships affected and the first that would make up a dazzling collection of great British liners in a two-month, strike-enforced lay-up in Southampton.

The strike cost Cunard an estimated £3¾ million through lost revenues, re-scheduling and re-coordinating of sailings, and, with the current losses then being experienced, brought the company's loss for the year to over £6m.

Sir Basil Smallpeice, (Cunard's chairman since November 1965 when he had succeeded Sir John Brocklebank on the latter's retirement through ill-health) decided the time had finally come for the drastic long-delayed surgery that the company so badly needed.

Sir John Brocklebank had, during his chairmanship, started a revolutionary policy of 'new thinking' which not only saw the cancellation of an intended replacement for the mighty *Queens* (a project known as the 'Q3' which later became known as the 'Q4' – the *Queen Elizabeth 2*) but also saw some of the other units of the fleet converted for cruising.

To this end two of Cunard's Canadian service ships, *Ivernia* and *Saxonia*, were converted for cruising in 1962, reappearing as the *Carmania* and *Franconia*. *Sylvania* and *Carinthia* would also be up-dated two years later with improvements being made to their passenger accommodation but with no change in name.

Not only were ships re-located in employment. The shore staff – for so long an almost separate organisation from the sea staff – was trimmed to meet the needs of a much reduced fleet.

Offices, too, were rationalised. Under Sir Basil's chairmanship many were closed, sold or transferred. The company headquarters was transferred from Liverpool to Southampton and many hitherto separated divisions came together under one roof.

Each department of Cunard had from now on to become a profitable, self-supporting unit – and this included the ships.

With the *Carmania* and *Franconia*, (painted in Cunard's cruising green) and with the *Mauretania* similarly employed, the company now had four ships (the *Caronia* being already employed in such a role) sailing the oceans of the world, chasing the sun in a trade that would expand spectacularly over the next two decades.

To meet the growing demand (and to reduce their winter losses) Cunard announced from New York in May 1962 that the *Queen Elizabeth* would be taken off the North Atlantic service for a month during the following winter and sent cruising. She would make three cruises from New York to Nassau and the 1,000 to 1,300 cruise passengers (2,200 were carried on normal voyages) would have their needs looked after by a specially appointed Cruise Director and a team of Social Directresses.

It was also in 1962 that the *Queens'* summer overhaul was dispensed with to effect further economies. As a result the liners would thereafter miss out on their fresh, summer coat of paint which had smartened up their gleaming hulls in readiness for the following high season.

The *Elizabeth* had some internal alterations made during the £450,000 1962 winter overhaul when a new cocktail bar was fitted, replacing the old Cabin Class

The 45 day Great Seamen's Strike of 1966 ended on 1st July 1966 and during that time many great British liners were laid up in idleness. Southampton's Western Docks presented a spectacular sight with (from left to right) *Windsor Castle, Queen Elizabeth, S.A. Vaal, Arcadia, Canberra, Good Hope Castle, Reina del Mar* and *Edinburgh Castle*. The strike accelerated the decline of the British Merchant Marine. *R. Bruce Grice*

Lounge. 150 Cabin Class staterooms and cabins were also furnished in new colour schemes, even having fitted carpets in lieu of the old carpet squares.

Sir John Brocklebank, then still chairman, described the *Queens* as 'the best hotels travelling between Southampton and New York' and more conversions were planned to maintain their premier position.

The first cruise of a *Queen* began on 21 February 1963 when the *Queen Elizabeth* made her first trip to the Caribbean since the war.

Sir John Brocklebank decided to cancel his booking for the first cruise, possibly due to the increasingly poor health which would ultimately lead to his resignation in 1965.

Two more cruises were announced for the first season, leaving New York on 28 February and 6 March respectively. The first cruise to Nassau was almost delayed by a tugmen's strike in New York but Commodore Watts undocked the ship without them.

On the liner's return the Commodore had to perform the trickier task of docking the ship, also unaided, which he did successfully. Two subsequent sailings and arrivals were performed under similar circumstances.

If the cruises of the *Elizabeth* proved to be successful, Cunard said, then both *Queens* would be sent cruising during the following season, with the *Queen Mary* cruising out of Southampton to the Atlantic Isles.

In March 1963 an anonymous telephone call to the New York Police warned of a bomb hidden on board the *Lizzie*. In spite of the limited search that was possible (because of the ship's enormous size) by both police and crew, nothing was found. It was probable that the hoax was perpetrated by frustrated 'union' activists.

The *QE* proved to be popular in her new role and as a consequence it was decided to make further interior improvements over the next few overhauls to suit her to the new market.

To this end, during the 1964 winter (January) refit, a new First Class Cocktail Bar was built in place of the under-used Promenade Deck Saloon. This new bar became known as the 'Midship Bar'. Decorated in dark green hide panels and colourful, contrasting furnishings of pink, dark green, gold and that popular colour of the 'Swinging '60s' – orange – the name and style of decor became very popular and would later find a complementary echo in the forthcoming Q4 – the *Queen Elizabeth 2*. A coral pink carpet – which surrounded a central dance floor – lay beneath a lowered ceiling that held aloft a glazed dome.

The same refit also saw two innovative rooms dedicated to teenaged travellers. The Teenagers' Room on the Main Deck was sited in a new structure placed under the new Lido swimming pool (but to the starboard of it) and aft of the old Cabin Lounge, now renamed the Caribbean Room. The Teenagers' Room contained a bowling alley,

The *Queen* berthed opposite to her usual quay. The Red Funnel tug *Vulcan*, also seen in the photograph, had a long and venerable career, having assisted the ill-fated White Star liner *Titanic* depart on her maiden voyage in 1912.

Dearden and Wade – now Thunder and Clayden – of Bournemouth/Queen Elizabeth Historical Society

Arrivals at terminus ports meant a great rush for luggage, porters and taxis. This shows one such arrival in New York.   *The University archives, the University of Liverpool*

A winter arrival in New York. Not only is there ice on the Hudson but the steam from the tugs has frozen on the ship's side. *The University Archives, the University of Liverpool*

football and car-racing tables, a cold drinks machine and the inevitable juke box.

Amongst the restyling for the new market the Cabin Class Restaurant became the Windsor Restaurant and the Cabin Smoking Room on the Promenade Deck became the Club Room for the new Lido.

The next refit (late 1964) saw soft furnishings fitted in all Main Deck suites.

The crew also benefited in a small way from the gradual, almost piecemeal (officially described as 'progressive') conversions for cruising.

The ship's men usually enjoyed a relaxing pint or two of beer in their off duty hours and a great deal of labour and space had been used in supplying the crew with adequate quantities of good English ale.

So far, 2,400 gallons of beer had been consumed by the crew on each round trip, the beverage being supplied via three to four hundred barrels containing between 5½ to 11 gallons per barrel. To cut down the intensive, unprofitable manpower required to load and unload the barrels, the cellar of the 'Pig and Whistle' was fitted with

nine tanks, each of 360 gallons capacity, in February 1965.

In that same month the Cunard decided that, if the *Queen* was to become completely viable as a cruise ship, large scale alterations had to be put in hand to make her more competitive with her rivals and more attractive to a public that was becoming increasingly aware of the pleasures of cruising, a growth industry that was to herald the resurrection of the giant passenger ship after a period of decline.

The alterations that would be carried out on the *Lizzie* would, it was anticipated in a news bulletin released for publication from the Cunard Building in Liverpool at 3 pm on Thursday 18 March, 'be spread over a four month period.'

Improvements to the liner would include the installation of full air-conditioning in both passenger and crew accommodation to help cope with the tropical climes into which the *Queen* was now being taken. Air-conditioning had hitherto been confined to the public rooms (for the liner's designated North Atlantic role) and the introduction of the system to the crews' accommodation was welcomed as their quarters on the Atlantic run had been, at best, stuffy. As a result of the alteration the *QE* changed from the unpopular ship that she had been (with some of the crew) to 'a much happier ship'.

To supply her with conditioned air, sixty four units were to be dotted about the ship in the vicinity of their associated Thermotanks. The existing Mail Room would be converted to house the refrigeration machinery.

Additional private showers and toilets were planned to be fitted in 250 Cabin-class and Tourist cabins, representing an increase of 230. 50 other rooms, already fitted with a toilet and shower, would also be supplied with a shower. A larger sea-water distillation plant would be installed to produce fresh water that would increase the *Queen*'s cruising range and a new decor would be created in all Tourist cabins which would also be furnished with fitted carpets in bright (but 'tasteful') colours.

The main structural change would involve the construction of a Lido area on the afterend of the Promenade Deck involving the erection of additional steel work extending aft to the Docking Bridge (these new screens would be emulated by the 'Q4') and the installation of an outdoor heated swimming pool as has been mentioned.

The contract for the conversion job – much to the chagrin of Southampton's shipyard unions – was awarded to the liner's original builders, John Brown and Co. (Clydebank) Ltd. The work would be carried out in the new graving dock in the Firth of Clyde which had been recently opened by the then Princess Royal.

The managing director of John Brown, John Rannie (later to be responsible for the building of the *QE2*), said in a news statement that welcomed the order (worth £1.5m):

'We are particularly pleased to receive this well balanced contract, providing work for all trades and ensuring continuity of employment for all our men when the Swedish American liner completes this year. The *Queen Elizabeth* will be in our hands from early next December to early March of next year, the three winter months, and will

During her conversion for cruising the Cunarder was dry-docked in the new facility on the Clyde.
George Outram & Co Ltd, Glasgow

employ on board at the Firth of Clyde Dry Dock, Greenock, over 2,500 men. 2,000 will be from Brown's of Clydebank, the remainder from the Dry Dock Company and the principal sub-contractors for the air conditioning plant, J. & E. Hall and Thermotank Ltd.

'This contract will provide work under good conditions for large numbers of joiners, plumbers, electricians and painters, at a time of year when employment is scarce. We believe it was awarded to us partly because of a satisfactory job done on the *Sylvania* this winter, and partly because the conversion is a large task to be completed in a short time and, having built the ship, we have the necessary data.

'Most of the steel work involved will be done by the Dry Dock Company and the engineering work by John Brown's engineers. We employ close on 6,000 men but could employ another 350, a few vacancies existing in all trades.'

Unfortunately the managing director's optimism would prove to be short-lived. The refit ran out of time with many jobs, especially in the new cabin areas on 'A' and 'C' decks which had not even been started, left undone. These would have to be completed in Southampton or even at sea.

The yard put the delay down to an epidemic of influenza amongst its workforce but Cunard considered that another vessel, three months behind its own schedule, had taken priority over their ship.

It was not only the delay in schedules that worried the Cunard people. Pilfering became a major cause for concern.

Not only did seven hundred brass bolts (amongst other items) intended for securing portholes disappear (apparently these had a "marketable" value in the dock road pubs of one pint for one bolt) but other non-ferrous items were pilfered that would have serious consequences long after the ship had left the Clyde.

With the fitting on board of so many new shower units and toilets – which would bring the *Elizabeth* up to a standard that was becoming expected by American travellers – there was a lot of copper piping about.

Sawn into short lengths this valuable piping could be smuggled out of the yard to become easily saleable scrap metal.

Not just content with taking scrap pieces of pipe, the pilferers would sometimes remove a covering panel concealing newly fitted pipe, scrape the paint to ascertain that it was copper and then drive a nail through to make sure that water was not already flowing through the length.

If the pipe was both copper and dry, then a saleable section would be sawn from it and the covering panel replaced.

As a result when water was later turned on as required (when the ship sailed from New York on her first cruise), cabins and corridors were flooded with water often appearing well away from its source.

Two days after the newly appointed Commodore Geoffrey Marr joined his ship (on March 7th), the liner left drydock on the first of two days of suitably high tides.

The blustery weather of the 9th was worrying but, as gales were forecast for the second day, the 25 knot gusts on the 9th were considered the lesser danger.

After an anxious journey down the Clyde (during which the pilot was convinced that the ship had twice lightly touched the bank because of the wind) the *Queen Elizabeth* reached the Tail O'the Bank where she anchored.

It was here that her reconditioned lifeboats, along with the new motor launches to be used as tenders during cruises, were to be taken on board – they had been left off for the journey downriver to help keep the liner's draught to a minimum. Lengthy attempts to hoist them on board had to be abandoned because of the weather but they were successfully embarked the next day.

Whilst the *Queen Elizabeth* was refitting on the Clyde many old hands who had built the ship took a pride in showing their children – and grandchildren – the beautiful ship that they had helped to create so many years before.

In spite of all the additional work that had been carried out on her the *Queen's* tonnage had been reduced during the refit to 82,998 tons gross. When she first appeared she had been near 84,000.

So it was with a certain nostalgic regret that the Clyde bade farewell to 'No. 552' as she sailed for Southampton. On board were many of John Brown's men travelling south in an attempt to finish the unaccomplished work. Many hundreds more headed south – by rail – with the same intent.

As the *Queen Elizabeth* sailed south she passed the Island of Bute on her starboard side. As she did so the

At sea in her element the *Queen Elizabeth* makes a marvellous sight in a turbulent sea.

Roger Sherlock collection

Commodore saluted octogenarian William McFarlane, who lived in retirement on the island, with a blast on the ship's whistle. McFarlane had been the shipyard manager in direct charge of building the great liner.

When she sailed from Southampton on Tuesday 29th March, the *Elizabeth* took thirty workmen with her to New York hoping to get the cabins on 'C' deck finished and the new cabins on 'D' deck started, their basic structure as yet un-erected.

On the uncompleted work Sir Basil Smallpeice commented 'It would be unrealistic to pretend that we are not disappointed – contractors and owners alike – that the whole of the work could not be finished on time. Much work had been carried out on time or ahead (of schedule) ...'

As has already been mentioned, shortly after the *Queen Elizabeth* sailed from New York where she had been given an enthusiastic – perhaps almost relieved – welcome, at the beginning of her first post-refit Caribbean cruise, floods occurred (due to the pillaged and damaged copper piping) with water three inches deep in eight cabins forward on 'C' deck. Carpets and curtains were quickly changed in the affected cabins and the rooms dried out: their temporarily displaced occupants returned to them apparently none-the-worse for their experience.

The cruise was nevertheless a great success.

After the cruise the *Queen* returned to the North Atlantic route, making a few crossings before the big strike of 1966. Although suffering heavy losses through the lay-up of their strike-bound fleet the company managed at least to achieve the completion of the cabins on 'D' deck, a task that could have possibly taken six months had the *QE* been at sea.

The strike over, the *Queen* sailed on Saturday 16th July, for the start of a short season of transatlantic voyages.

On 21st September the *QE* started her first long cruise from New York. Gales followed the ship from Bermuda all the way to Lisbon, a call at the Azores was cancelled, a short cruise around the island being undertaken instead. Tangier was also omitted because of the wind and a large sea swell in the harbour, but from Madeira to Dakar and back across the Atlantic to the Caribbean it was sunshine all the way with the storms and the disappointment of ports missed soon being forgotten.

The new air-conditioning had worked well in the recently fitted cabins but the public rooms were stifling and many events were held in the open air. Although when the liner was built the public rooms had been fitted with what had been, at the time, thought of as remarkable air-conditioning, it had been designed to operate on sea temperature, which meant the coolness of the North Atlantic.

But in the tropics, the temperature of the sea rose to 80-90°F and as a result the rooms became almost untenable. However, an adjustment back in Southampton brought the new plants spare capacity into play and the problem was solved. Further extensions to the system were made during the winter overhaul of November 1966.

In October of the same year a tugmen's strike in Southampton found the *Queen* stranded in Cherbourg, unable to reach her home port. Passengers were tendered back to England but a group of stewards who joined the tender in order to reach home to get their cruising whites for the cruise that was to follow were ordered back on the *Lizzie* by the Master-At-Arms as all shore leave had been cancelled.

A nasty situation was averted when the men were allowed to fly home. The company gave an assurance through the union/ship liaison group (the *QE* was the first ship to have such a group, organised after the Seaman's Strike) that such an occurrence would not happen again, as catering, engineering and female staff had walked off the ship in sympathy. (The union liaison group had, amongst other things, negotiated for corned beef to be supplied for the crew as a homely change to the rich food provided. It never reached the crew as apparently the officers and pursers 'commandeered' it!)

The subsequent winter cruises to the West Indies were poorly patronised and, as had already been described, one of the series was cancelled and replaced with an unscheduled North Atlantic voyage.

This also suffered from low bookings and was known as the 'Ghost Ship Voyage'. It was also costly to the company especially through the oil fuel required to maintain the required fast passage.

The short cruises to Nassau from New York took one and a half days each way with a similar length of time being spent ashore. On one cruise a sudden storm hit the area and the *QE* had to sail round to the lee of the island leaving two hundred pleasure seekers stranded ashore to sleep 'rough in a barn'. They returned to the ship the following morning.

The short cruises of that season were followed by another extended cruise to the Mediterranean, the *Queen Elizabeth* sailing on Tuesday February 21st (1967). The liner was scheduled to visit fourteen ports in thirty seven days, arriving back in New York on Thursday March 30th.

The idea was good but the Commodore kept to himself his reservations that it was the wrong time of year for such a long cruise.

A total of fifty-eight shore excursions had been arranged by American Express who had their own office on board (the crew had their own tours arranged for one third the price) ranging from a few hours ashore for $6 to six day extended tours for $416. These latter tours would take the lucky passengers from the ship (anchored off Alexandria) to places such as Cairo, Aswan, Luxor, Jerusalem, Bethlehem, Baalbek, the Dead Sea, Damascus etc. before rejoining the liner at the then lovely city of Beirut.

From Las Palmas and Gibraltar the *Queen* headed towards North Africa but for the second time a half-day call at Tangier was cancelled because of yet another heavy swell. However, the promise of a complete day in Palma on the island of Majorca was well received by the passengers.

Shortly after midnight after leaving Majorca the ship was put around in a heavy sea that had been whipped up by a strong WNW gale. A crew member was reported overboard.

Only a perfunctory search could be carried out because of the weather conditions so, after two hours, a message was sent to other ships requesting them to keep a lookout for the missing man. Apparently he had been depressed, had been drinking heavily and had deliberately jumped overboard.

The *Queen Elizabeth* found the sea conditions at Alexandria too rough to effect any landings. After consulting Cunard in Southampton and obtaining reluctant permission to rearrange the itinerary (and to spend an extra £20,000 in fuel!) Commodore Marr asked the American Express people on board to re-schedule the next few days of tours.

All this resulted in the *Queen* diverting to Athens (which would have come later in the cruise anyway) and then dashing back to Alexandria where the planned complex series of tours could belatedly go ahead.

After three days at Alexandria the *QE* then went on to Beirut (where she picked up her passengers from the extended tours) then headed west to Messina. The call at Rhodes was omitted in order to make up time. Athens had already been visited.

Naples, Cannes, Barcelona, Lisbon and Madeira (where crew members swopped old pairs of shoes for wicker chairs etc bartered from the local 'bum boats') followed before the ship headed once again for New York where she arrived in the afternoon of Thursday 30th March, thus completing a very successful cruise as far as the passengers were concerned.

The Commodore, however, had slipped on a patch of spilt detergent shortly after leaving Madeira and suffered a 'dislocated right ankle, a fractured fibia and a cracked tibia'.

He handed over command to his Staff Captain, George Smith, and it was whilst the Commodore was home on sick leave that the axe fell.

The *Queen Mary* had been scheduled to be phased out in 1968 with the *Queen Elizabeth* carrying on in partnership with the new Q4, for a year at least.

But the letters that were opened concurrently on board both liners on 8th May 1967 said differently. Captain William Law was in command of the *Lizzie* on the poignant occasion. He later told the press 'It will be awful to say good-bye to this magnificent ship. It has been an honour to command her.'

In spite of her recent expensive refit and her gradual progression into profitability the *Queen Elizabeth* was to be withdrawn a year earlier than had been anticipated, just a year after the *Queen Mary*'s retirement.

The news was stunning, not least to Commodore Marr. It had been arranged that he would remain with his flagship until after the introduction of 'Q4' (the *Queen Elizabeth 2*) and run his vessel in conjunction with the 'New Cunarder', providing a vestige of the old two ship service.

Captain 'Bil' Warwick would have command of the new liner.

But the news meant not only the early retirement of the great ship, but also the early retirement of Commodore Marr who would also have to take a proportionate cut in pension!

On the same day the letters were opened on board the two *Queens*, Sir Basil Smallpeice said:

'Although the *Queen Mary*'s retirement next year had long been forecast, it had been hoped that the results of the *QE*'s cruise programme last winter would confirm the viability of the company's plan to keep her in service when the 'Q4' came along in 1969. In the event, the results had been very far from satisfactory. The board's decision to withdraw her and the *QM* is part of the unrelenting process of facing realities in their determination to put the company on to a paying basis.'

Recently introduced legislation by IMCO (International Maritime Commission) also influenced the company's decision. The Americans demanded that the *Queen* be brought up to the new standards of fire-protection which would have to include the fitting of additional fire-sprinklers and the boxing-in of stairways that could otherwise act as deadly draught tunnels in the event of fire.

The work, Cunard estimated, would cost £750,000 but would keep the *QE* on the Atlantic for a few more years running in conjunction with the 'New Cunarder'.

However, the U.S. legislators had another surprise up their sleeve. When Cunard requested that the Americans sent over an inspector to approve the improvement work as it progressed the authorities declined. The Americans wanted the work on the ship completed and then send her over to New York for inspection prior to approval and certification.

This would mean an empty, expensive trip to New York and, if the inspection failed, an equally expensive return trip back to the U.K. for the work that would then be needed to bring the liner up to requirements. Added to this there was also the loss of revenue.

In total, the prospect to Cunard was too daunting and contributed greatly to their decision to dispose of the *Queen*.

As soon as the decision to retire the *Queen* was made public the *QE*'s cruises and Atlantic liner voyages became popular with those who had travelled on and had loved the ship over the length of her career; the ship started to make a profit. On occasion a hand-made 'For Sale' notice would appear on the dockside or through a porthole as crew and passengers tried to make the point that Britain's heroic heritage was about to be auctioned off to the highest bidder.

The *Queen* made a few Atlantic crossings in between her winter cruises but the weather encountered during her northern voyages left her paintwork rather too dishevelled for her cruising role.

By this time special offers were made available in England for people to travel to Cherbourg by regular ferry and then join one of the *Queens* on the short trip to Southampton.

The enthusiastic Channel travellers often had the huge public rooms to themselves when the liner travelled overnight. Daylight brought a dismal view.

Large tarpaulins had been erected over the decking aft of the *Lizzie*'s funnels in an attempt to keep the wood planking free of the smuts that exuded from the less-than-pristine stacks. But grime found its way under the covers, themselves grimy from the falling soot.

The *Queen*, it seemed, was tired and only waiting to go.

Ever since the announcement of her impending redundancy within the future plans of Cunard, the once proud liner seemed ready to slip into oblivion.

Scrapping seemed to provide the obvious, almost humane, answer for exiting the world stage especially after such a magnificently full career. But many thought the *Lizzie* should be preserved in Southampton as the *Mary* had been in Long Beach, California.

The *Queen Mary* had been fortunate in finding a buyer in the form of the City of Long Beach for which port she had left Southampton on October 31st 1967.

In the last years of her own career the *Mary* had cruised from Southampton to the Atlantic Isles just as the *Lizzie* had cruised from New York to the Caribbean.

The two great liners met for the last time when they were both at sea. Just after midnight on 25th September 1967, the *Queens* passed each other in mid Atlantic, the *Queen Mary* en route to Southampton for the last time. Lights illuminating five funnels flashed on and off in a mutual salute as Captain Treasure Jones on the retiring ship and Captain Marr on the *Elizabeth* doffed their caps from their positions on their respective Bridge wings. Within a few short minutes the plans, hopes and successes of three decades came to an end as sirens boomed out across the water, the whole poignant scene witnessed by a few passengers braving the night wind.

Now, in a great blaze of publicity, the *QM* left Southampton on what was billed as 'The Last Great Cruise' which included a passage through the Magellan Straits taking her around the notorious Cape Horn to California.

She is still at Long Beach and, rumourdly after two changes in management, seems likely to continue her life as an entertainment and business complex under the aegis of the Disney empire.

Spurred on by the £1.5 million they had received for the *Mary* the company now looked to get a better price for the second of the 'set', so over the months that followed the announcement of her forthcoming disposal Cunard received many offers for their ageing – but still yacht like and beautiful – flagship that now seemed almost too big for anyone to do anything with.

But the bids came in and, between September 1967, and the following March, Cunard had received serious enquiries from many quarters.

The Japanese wanted her for a marine science museum in time for the 1970 Tokyo World Fair. Honolulu was interested as were the Australians. Mexico wanted her as an attraction in Acapulco where the *Queen Mary* had been well received en-route to Long Beach. Brazil wanted her for a gambling den.

Sir Howard Pitman was interested in the ship for use as a huge emigrant carrier to Australia and even good old Britain said why not keep her for British holiday makers?

Evangelist Dr. Billy Graham offered £2.083 million for her to become a floating Bible School and the United States

Institute of Technology wanted her for a floating university.

Six actual offers for the liner came from approximately one hundred enquiries and on 5th April 1968, Cunard announced the successful bidder.

For $7.75 million (£3.23 million) *Queen Elizabeth* was won by a group of Philadelphian businessmen who planned to moor her off Hog Island in their Pennsylvanian Delaware river. Delivery would take place sometime after the liner had completed her very last cruise on 15th November.

Charles Willard, one of the three men whose company had won the ship, said in the words of a royal suitor:

'We Americans have turned to your great nation so often for inspiration and instruction. We now come to obtain one of your prized possessions. Be sure the *Queen Elizabeth* will be welcomed and cared for in the fashion her long and illustrious career in war and peace warrants.'

In deference to the 'New Cunarder' the liner would be renamed *The Elizabeth*.

But two months later the purchasers with their $25 million plan ran into difficulties one of which (perhaps with hindsight) had been strangely obvious – the Delaware River was not deep enough! Even more strangely, perhaps, Cunard had not sent a representative to check that the Philadelphia site was at all suitable.

Added to this the State of Pennsylvania budget had been so cut that the planned highway to the ship would not be built for at least another four or five years.

However, a new site had been found for the liner – fast becoming a pawn in a giant game of real-estate politics – at Fort Lauderdale in Florida.

Two of the three buyers pose by the liner's binnacle.
Philadelphia Magazine

The *Queen*, meanwhile, carried on sailing almost like 'a cheap store that has huge notices outside which say Final Closing Down Sale more or less permanently displayed' as Geoffrey Marr recalled. He considered that the *Queen Elizabeth*'s retirement had been announced far too early for decency.

The liner's last cruises from New York were successes with the ship sailing to ports which could actually accommodate her. The mis-placed winter North Atlantic voyages that interspersed the cruises were less than well patronised – and the weather tended to spoil the paintwork for cruising. The high speed Atlantic dashes also lost money because of the heavy fuel consumption that was required to maintain express timetables.

Happily the *Queen*'s final summer season was financially successful as many old friends of the ship travelled on a last nostalgic journey.

But her slight turn in fortune came too late to affect any change in the decisions that had emanated from the Cunard Boardroom a few months previously. The 'New thinking' of the Board could not be dissuaded from its course of reform.

The *Queen Elizabeth*'s final season on the Atlantic was uneventful other than for the enthusiasms expressed by her old passengers from the years of peace and war, and who wanted to travel on her for just one last time.

Sailing from Southampton on 12th September the liner carried a large scale model of her successor – the *Queen Elizabeth 2* – at that moment completing her own fitting out on the Clyde.

The *Lizzie* left Southampton at the outset of her last voyage on October 23rd. Sadly this was marred by a tug dispute but the liner managed to make the tide at the Brambles and her sailing was not delayed.

Because of the uncertain financial and organisational condition of the liner's new owners, an announcement was made by Cunard which coincided with the *Queen*'s last sailing from Southampton to New York.

The company stepped in to moderate a worsening situation by more or less taking over the new venture themselves. Injecting $1 million into a new company called 'The Elizabeth (Cunard) Corporation' – of which they would have control with an 85% share – Cunard hoped that their continuing involvement with the *Queen Elizabeth* would reap worthwhile dividends in the years to come.

The three Philadelphians, however, still held a small interest in the company and would lease the ship from Cunard for $2 million a year. They would also have the option of completely taking over the ship after a period of ten years.

Sir Basil Smallpeice for Cunard said that the new agreement would benefit his company considerably. 'Once the project is underway' he told the press 'it should be capable of generating its own finance' adding that the new contract would enable Cunard to retain control of the policy and development of the *Elizabeth* Corporation for as long as Cunard wished.

On board the liner the Commodore told a gathering of four hundred crew members that the company would still be retaining an active interest in the liner's future role after her retirement. The meeting cheered him to a man.

The centre of all of the speculation arrived in New York for the last time on Monday, 28th October, to a series of farewell tributes that would put her home port of Southampton to shame.

Before she sailed on her final departure from her New York home the *Queen Elizabeth* was feted and honoured with both private and official functions being held on board.

The English Speaking Union held a $100-a-head dinner with guests being piped on board by the Glen Eagle Highlanders pipe band.

Mayor John Lindsay boarded the liner on the 30th, sailing day, to bid an official farewell. Presenting the ship with a plaque from the Department of Defence to commemorate the liner's remarkable war service, Mayor Lindsay said 'Today we can say 'The *Queen* is dead, long live the *Queen*' because in three months time the Cunard Steamship Company will bring into New York the splendid new flagship, the *Queen Elizabeth 2*'.

As the crew called 'Last call, all ashore' for the very last time the band played 'Auld Lang Syne' as the crowd of visitors was reluctantly ushered towards the gangway.

So on Wednesday 30th October the *Lizzie* sailed, finally, from New York. Responding with three blasts on her mighty sirens she replied to each of the decorated small craft that tooted their own tributes as they accompanied her, wake-like, on her journey down the River Hudson to the open sea.

Commodore Geoffrey Marr's lasting memory of the event had been received in a letter. Writing on 22nd October, L.W. Douglas, one time American ambassador to the Court of St James (his daughter would be travelling on the last trip on honeymoon), eloquently summed up the worth of the *Queen Elizabeth* and her sister:

'My Dear Commodore Marr:

'On the Eve of the *Queen Elizabeth*'s last voyage to her native shores it is fitting that the people of the Western World should be reminded of the indispensable role that she and her older sister, the *Queen Mary*, played in the last great worldwide convulsion.

'For almost three years, these two Sovereigns of the Seas silently sped across the waters of the North Atlantic, carrying with them more than two million fighting men from this continent to join the soldiers of the English-Speaking world who had fought so gallantly (and were to continue to engage so successfully) the evil forces that Hitler had unleashed on the world.

'In the darkness of the night, each of the great ships would quietly slip into the sheltering harbours of the Clyde or New York and, within less than seventy-two hours, in the greyness of the dawn, or the blackness of midnight, unheralded and unsung, would vanish into the vast spaces of the Atlantic, to run the gauntlet of the hostile German wolfpacks awaiting them. Unescorted, except during the last few miles of each voyage, their speed, and the skilful command of their officers, enabled them successfully to elude the vigilant enemy that would have sent them to the bottom of the ocean.

'Each ship made two round trips a month. During every summer month, when the North Atlantic was less boisterous, together they carried almost 70,000 soldiers to fight for freedom in England and in Europe; during each of the winter months, when the seas were apt to be more turbulent, they lifted almost 62,000 men in uniform to the white cliffs of Southern England.

'There is in history a chain of events that, as the first link is welded, leads on to others. So it is in the case of these two noble ships.

'Had it not been for Sir Percy Bates' determination to cause the *Queens* to be constructed and to slip down their ways into the Clyde; had they not been available to move more than two million American troops across the North Atlantic; had these troops not been assembled in Britain for the cross channel operation 'Overlord' in June of 1944, there would have been no invasion of Normandy, and the 'buzz-bomb' launching pads on the European continent would not have been captured in time to save London from being reduced to a pile of rubble.

'The two great *Queens* thus soldered the chain which was to frustrate Hitler's ambition to obliterate the basic freedoms of the civilized world.

'And so – as you guide the last of the two matchless *Queens* on her final voyage, will you bid her an affectionate and reverent 'ave atque vale' from those in this troubled world who owe so much to their uninterrupted and glorious contribution to the cause of free men, everywhere.

'They have merited a high place on the roster of the world's immortals.

'One generation succeeds another. Soon another *Queen* will replace the one we now salute. She will carry on the unfinished task of binding the Old World closer to the New.

L. W. Douglas'

The Commodore had the text of the letter typed out and pinned on the crews' notice board.

At sea, on Sunday 3rd November, to mark the *Queen Elizabeth*'s final North Atlantic Eastbound crossing, the Commodore held a Farewell Dinner.

After a journey that was remembered as being particularly happy the last night out was understandably a poignant and emotional occasion. At the end of the evening's entertainment as a large a crowd as possible of passengers and crew (including the Commodore) poured onto the dance floor for a heart-felt rendition of that traditional song of farewell by Robert Burns, 'Auld Lang Syne'.

Among the passengers were Lord and Lady Montague of Beaulieu and Jack Frost, journalist and a lifetime devotee of the *Queen*. He had co-authored, with Neil Potter, a magnificent tribute to the liner, 'The Elizabeth', published a few years before in 1965.

Frankie Howerd, the British comedian, was also on board and had entertained the passengers during the trip.

The last crossing was described as ' .... a gala trip .... one of the best crossings we've had' as when, on 4th November 1968, the liner arrived in Southampton coming to the end of the career for which she had been designed.

It was the end of Voyage 495. She had crossed the Atlantic 896 times; she had carried over the years 2,300,000 passengers (excluding her war service) and had steamed 3,472,672 miles in the service of the nation that had so

The Queen Mother, accompanied by Commodore Marr, surveys the ship from the advantage of a Bridge wing.

Commodore Geoffrey Marr chats to H.M. as she wistfully holds the wheel that she held during the liner's trials in 1946. Sir Basil Smallpeice listens in during this final Royal visit to the ship that the Queen Mother had also launched.
Both photos Southern Newspapers plc, Southampton

proudly given the ship her being and had latterly made 31 cruises.

The advent of her last transatlantic arrival in the Hampshire port (an hour late due to bad weather) turned out to be a quiet affair, the occasion lacking the thousands of spectators that the similar arrival of the *Queen Mary* had commanded. The *Lizzie* gave three blasts on her siren.

As the liner pulled alongside Berth 107 in the New (Western) Docks the Commodore on the Bridge became anxious as the prevailing wind tried to blow the *Queen Elizabeth* away from the quay and at the way that a couple of mooring lines were being handled. Picking up his amplified megaphone he roared out 'Heave away for'd!'

Hearing the admonition from above him a wag on a lower bridge front deck recalled Frankie Howerd's referring to the Commodore as a 'god' during a cabaret act during the voyage (the comedian had got Geoffrey Marr's permission 'to take the mickey' out of him) and called out 'Has God spoken?' The tension was broken.

It had been announced earlier that the day following the last arrival, on 6th November, Her Majesty the Queen Mother would visit the liner to pay her own tribute to the Pride of Britain that she had launched thirty years previously.

In readiness for the Royal visit the shoreside paintwork of the liner's superstructure and funnel was scrubbed and cleaned. The omission of a summer overhaul, a stormy North Atlantic and the breakdown of a couple of forced draught fans had given the liner a rather too grubby an appearance.

Internally the woodwork and metalwork was polished until it gleamed. By the time the flower and plant arrangements with which British Rail had decorated the terminal building had found an echo in 'R' Deck Square where the Queen Mother would embark the ship's company had a ship of which they could be justly proud.

Just before noon on the appointed day Her Majesty stepped on board, having arrived from London by train. The Queen Mother was met by Commodore Marr and Staff Captain W. J. Law. She then chatted to the crew members who formed the guard of honour before being taken up to the Midships Bar where senior officers and senior company representatives awaited to be presented.

Lunch followed (Dover Sole followed by Saddle of Southdown Lamb all washed down with Chateau Lafite Rothschild '59 and, the Royal favourite, Batard Montrachet '62), after which Sir Basil Smallpeice presented the Queen Mother with one of the limited edition goblets specially engraved as keepsakes for the crew. In response the Royal guest thanked everybody and made expressions of her close interest in the liner's career as it had gradually unfolded over the years.

The *Queen*'s journey into history was approaching fulfilment but in a way less grand, less magnificent and even less dignified than suited her position.

Geoffrey Marr then conducted the Queen Mother on a tour of the ship during which she met, at her own request, as many of the 'old' Cunard hands as she could. The tour included a visit to the open areas of the Promenade Deck and Bridge where the feathers of Her Majesty's hat blew in the lively breeze of the fading autumnal afternoon of what had been a bright, sunny day.

During the course of the tour the Commodore and his regal guest had discussed her portrait painted by Sir Oswald Birley that hung in the Main Lounge. It was the commissioning of this portrait that had caused so much controversy just after the war, over twenty years previously.

After the Queen Mother had stepped ashore for the very last time the Commodore was able to reflect on the events of the day.

At lunch the Queen Mother had asked him about the future plans for the ship after her arrival in Florida. Her Majesty 'expressed the hope that the end of the liner's life would be in line with the same proud tradition she had maintained in both peace and war'.

Geoffrey Marr, however, was not so hopeful but 'kept my forebodings to myself'.

The beginning of the final act. Almost 'stealing away' the Queen Elizabeth edges away from her final berth.   *Cedric Wasser*

His doubts, especially about the future financial security of the ship, had been fuelled by an article he had read in the June edition of the American magazine, 'Philadelphia'.

This reputable publication had been approached in mid-May by Stanton Miller, one of the trio of the successful bidders for the *Queen Elizabeth*, to write an article about the liner's forthcoming arrival in Philadelphia in order to help persuade the City to release more land for car parking; to point out the advantages of having the liner as the city's 'newest landmark' (as a Cunard advert had referred to the ship during the *Queen*'s final season); and to try to rekindle some enthusiasm for the project in the local press.

The 'Philadelphia' editorial stated that it had '... assigned one of our writers to do a piece on the ship and the deal,' but added ominously 'The story he brought back .... was not the story he went after.' The reporter wrote an article that '.... raises more questions than it answers.'

The three business men, brothers Robert and Stanton Miller along with their partner Charles Williard (the three of whom collectively liked to be known as 'C-B-S') '.. were known' the editorial continued, 'to this magazine' from previous investigations.

The Millers were, it was claimed '... closely associated with people to whom this publication is an anathema' referring to the brothers' dealings with the Teamsters Union in various business arrangements that 'smelt' badly of Mafia involvement.

Williard, president of a large electrical contract firm, had been attacked by the magazine a year previously for '.... playing funny games with a free wheeling labor boss.'

It also transpired that two eminently unqualified persons had carried out the 'careful investigations' on behalf of C-B-S to ensure that the planned locale for the

Almost stealing away into the mist on the morning that she left Britain forever the *Queen* was watched by very few spectators.   *Author's collection*

Queen's final berthing place in the Delaware River was suitable for the task. These 'experts' failed to show an insufficient depth of water (the river would need expensive dredging); they failed to investigate the possible hazard that could be caused to low-flying aircraft flying to and from Philadelphia's international airport; they failed to note the noise pollution caused by aircraft every few minutes and they failed to report on the pollution caused by odours emanating from the nearby oil-refinery.

The Philadephian trio soon thereafter decided that their

city was not, after all, geared-up for their ambitious venture. Using the lack of roads to connect their site to the main highway as an excuse they decided that perhaps Florida would make a more appropriate site for their acquisition.

Financial difficulties followed as C-B-S found that they were unable to raise the balance of the agreed purchase price for their gigantic piece of floating hardware.

Their hopes, and the hopes of those people who perhaps shared the 'Philadelphia's point of view that their city had within their grasp '... an unparalleled opportunity for them and for the city ..', an opportunity that '... must not be lost ...', were dashed as the prospect of millions of dollars' worth of tourism and conventions faded from view. Philadelphia felt jilted.

However, in New York, Cunard's negotiators still spoke of C-B-S as 'extremely gracious people'!

No wonder the Commodore felt uneasy!

On the evening of 7th November the crew held their own farewell dance in a Southampton ballroom to which Commodore and Mrs. Marr had been invited as guests of honour.

The crew had all contributed to make a presentation to their captain. This took the form of a heavy, solid silver rosebowl inscribed:

'RMS *Queen Elizabeth*, 2nd (sic) November 1968. Presented by the Ships Company on the last voyage to Commodore Geoffrey Marr DSC RD RNR. In appreciation of his unfailing thoughtfulness and his many timely arrivals.'

The 'unfailing thoughtfulness' and 'many timely arrivals' referred to, recalled the Commodore's earnest attempts to dock the *Queen Elizabeth* in Southampton – often ahead of schedule – so that crew members going ashore could catch the last bus or train home to their families or perhaps get to their favourite pub before closing time!

Geoffrey Marr, even now in 1989, still relishes the sentiments expressed with great amusement and still appreciates what had generally been a good and loyal crew.

The day following the dance and presentation saw the *Queen Elizabeth* sailing on her ultimate cruise of farewell. This would take her to Las Palmas and Gibraltar. To the strains of Southampton's Salvation Army band playing the *de-rigeur* 'Auld Lang Syne', she slipped into Southampton Water, the prelude of her commercial swan-song.

The cruise gave a small part of Britain a chance to voice its regret as her passing, a chance that would again put the mother-land to shame.

As the liner left Gibraltar she was escorted by a flotilla of ships of the Royal Navy. Before they turned away for 'Gib' they steamed by and saluted the *Queen* as she gradually built up speed. Jet fighters roared overhead. Geoffrey Marr recalled 'It was a wonderful farewell. The dreadful thought behind it was that it was farewell.'

The *Queen Elizabeth* arrived back at Berth 107 in Southampton Docks an hour late, again because of a high wind, on Friday 15th November. That evening the crew paid off. Some would join the *QE2*, a few (193) would sail with the *Lizzie* to her new home but the rest found themselves 'on the beach' after many years of loyal service.

On 18th November the last function to be held on board was a dance held for nine hundred serving and ex-officers and for senior local dignitaries. The occasion was over subscribed and, because the ship's company had been dismissed, an outside firm of caterers provided the refreshment. The evening combined regret that the largest liner the world had ever seen was passing from the oceans with a thankful feeling that the ship's life had been well lived.

But the future of the *Queen Elizabeth*, even at this late hour, was still uncertain as she slipped away from England in the early morning fog of a dull 28th November.

As the ship sailed the Commodore's wife, daughter, the ever loyal Jack Frost and a handful of officials had to be landed by tug. The liner had slipped her moorings a little sooner than had been anticipated because only half the usual number of seamen were on board attempting to cope with casting off the mooring lines.

Other than for Southampton's Albion Band the quayside was almost bereft of well-wishers. The *Queen Elizabeth* was almost slinking away under the cover of the fog. Mrs Marr recalled the departure as 'a disgrace'. Her opinion was shared by many who compared the sailing as being diametrically opposite to the grand farewell given to the *Queen Mary*.

Later, Geoffrey Marr wrote badly of the sailing comparing it to the farewells given to the ship in New York and Gibraltar. He described it as '... a British understatement with a vengeance, as though the British world of ships and shiplovers looked the other way until she had gone!'

The other ships that were in Southampton that unhappy morning saluted the *Queen Elizabeth* as she passed by but received no acknowledgement to their respectful signals. A temporary electrical fault had developed with the *Lizzie*'s whistle control gear and she left the port in a silence that only added to the almost furtive feeling of the departure.

As the *Lizzie* made her silent passage through the Solent and Spithead she was cheered by the ship's company of HMS *Hampshire*, one of the Royal Navy's class of guided missile destroyers.

Passing down through the Channel later that evening the homeward-bound cruising Cunarder *Carmania* made her own farewells to her giant sister.

Queen Elizabeth 2, the 'New Cunarder', also sent a message of good wishes for the future success of her predecessor as the former liner underwent her own initially successful trials off the Isle of Arran. A month later disaster would strike the *QE2* on her prolonged trials to the Canaries – a disaster that would take many months to resolve and would even cast a shadow on her future role with Cunard.

For the *Queen Elizabeth* steaming towards a new life in Florida it was the end of an honourable, wonderful, prosperous and often glamorous career.

But it was not yet to be the end of the ship that was once RMS *Queen Elizabeth*.

Two aerial studies of the liner show the *Queen Elizabeth* passing by Weston and Netley (above) and Fawley oil refinery (below) as she leaves Southampton Water for the last time. The two photographs graphically show the 'spit and polish' applied to the starboard side of the liner in preparation for the Queen Mother's visit whilst the port side remains stained from her final voyages.

Reproduced by kind permission of FotoFlite, Ashford, Kent

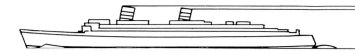

Chapter Thirteen

'... The most Mighty of Pyres ... the Roaring Flames Mingled with Weeping ...'

('Beowulf')

As a postscript, the last years of the liner were far from the honourable time that many had hoped for her but they must be related in order to complete the saga of the ship which had once been the *Queen Elizabeth*.

The first inkling that the officials of the cities of Fort Lauderdale and Hollywood in Broward County, Florida, had that the liner was to be retired in their shared harbour of Port Everglades (instead of Philadelphia) came in January 1968.

Late that month Mayor-Commissioner Edmund R. Burry wrote 'It has come to my notice that there is a possibility of situating the *Queen Elizabeth* in Port Everglades on a permanent basis.

By June, after much discussion and local argument about who would pay for road access to the liner, water supply, sewage, police and fire services, etc, the two cities were still enthusiastic. Commissioner Al Hines wrote to William Skillings, whose public relations firm was doing much of the planning: 'It was encouraging and most flattering for all of Hollywood's city officials to learn this week that the *Queen Elizabeth* will be located at Port Everglades as opposed to the many cities and nations who were interested.

'... thank you for the effort you have expended in keeping excitement at a fever pitch ...'. Director James Beattie of Hollywood's Publicity Department wrote that its advertising advisory board was:

A view of the *Elizabeth* alongside what would become the passenger terminal in Port Everglades. One can only wonder as to her success as a hotel etc had she remained there to enjoy the port's later rise to a premier cruise port.   *Peter Walters*

'... your proposal would certainly be well received by this community.

'... I am convinced that the placement of this great vessel will benefit us immeasurably.'

The Mayor-Commissioner then went on to envisage the liner '... retaining a British atmosphere ...' and that he would be 'opposed to allowing such a great ship being degraded in any manner.'

'... completely overwhelmed at the decision ..'

Even by the time that the *Elizabeth* was on her last cruise to Gibraltar the two cities still expected that the liner would be with them sometime during the new year. It was fully expected also that Cunard would want much of the conversion work to be done in Britain which would give Broward County ample time to prepare the site and its services.

Under her own steam at last and almost looking her old self, *Seawise University* makes a cautionary call at Rio en-route to Hong Kong.
Collection of Robert Lenzer, Richardson, Texas

Everybody must have been surprised when it was announced that the liner would be arriving off the Florida coast early in December.

After a ghost-like voyage that took her diagonally across the North Atlantic, the liner arrived off Boco Raton on Saturday 7th December. Dredging had not been completed in Port Everglades so the Commodore was told to cruise the ship down the coast to show the flag, which he did. Slowly sailing as far south as Key Biscayne her progression was watched by thousands of spectators during the day, thrilled by the sight and sound of the magnificent ship, and by many thousands more at night who marvelled at the beauty of a liner bejewelled by hundreds of lights, as others had marvelled before them.

Heading north from Key Biscayne the *Queen Elizabeth* spent the night of 7-8th December steaming around the ocean off Fort Lauderdale, waiting for her triumphant entry into the port early the next morning.

At 11.15 on the morning of the 8th after the ship had berthed, Commodore Marr rang that final, often fatal, order on the Bridge telegraph to the Engine Room:

'Finished with Engines.'

Shortly after arrival the Commodore received a cryptic cable from Captain Storey, Cunard's nautical adviser in Southampton: 'For Commodore Marr in *QE* on arrival. Acts 27 Verse 39 (signed) Storey.'

Looking up the reference quoted in the Holy Bible, the Commodore found the passage 'And when it was day, they knew not the land: but they discovered a certain creek with a shore, into which they were minded, if it were possible, to thrust in the ship.'

It was in this 'certain creek' of Port Everglades that the liner would remain for two years.

Initially response to the presence of the *Elizabeth* – the ship that was the *Queen Elizabeth* – (the prefix *Queen* had been dropped at Cunard's request) was good after the liner opened to the public on 14th February 1969, but finance and local politics soon took a hand.

The old Cunard hands who had been interviewed by Stanton Miller to stay with the ship to act as guides and advisers were later reduced in number from 120 to 30 (mostly engineers who had been retained to assist in running boilers and generators). Some men who had sailed her over had returned home after the ship's arrival. Others would return after the ship's later sale to Queen Ltd.

A few months after the ship's opening, the liner was

again up for sale. Offers came from all over the world: £3 million from a concern wanting to operate the *Elizabeth* between the United Kingdom and Australia; the Charter Travel Club offered £1.7 million and another bid was made by Puerto Rican interests.

The successful bid for the liner came in July when the ship that had been the *Queen Elizabeth* was sold for $8.64 million to Queen Ltd. a subsidiary of Utility Leasings in which the old trio of C-B-S had an interest.

It was whilst under the new ownership that a hurricane warning caused the by then almost deserted ship to be partially scuttled to prevent her, it was feared, tearing away from her berth.

Deserted and by now almost unwanted, the neglected liner, once the pride of Britain's merchant marine, was once more put up for auction. Queen Ltd. was bankrupt with debts of $12 million.

The notice of sale proclaimed that the liner would be offered 'free and clear of liens and encumbrances' whilst the catalogue listed forty lots that would come under the hammer. The sale would be held at the Galt Ocean Mile Hotel, Fort Lauderdale, between 9th and 10th September 1970.

The lots on offer included furniture from crew and passenger areas; radar and compass equipment; liferafts; oil paintings; a tapestry, and many other fittings. The apparel of a great ship would be dispersed piecemeal, unless a single buyer could be found for the entire ship and its contents.

A representative of the Island Navigation Company of Hong Kong made an almost last-minute but successful bid of $3.2 million (£1.33 million). The Island Navigation Company (to be responsible for moving and repairing the ship) was in turn a subsidiary of the giant Orient Overseas Line also of Hong Kong which would be the liner's actual owner and operator. This enormous shipping empire, which contained much well-looked-after second-hand tonnage within its fleet, was owned by Mr C.Y. Tung. Described as a dynamic, jolly, man his interests incorporated tankers, bulk carriers, and car ferries as well as passenger liners.

Mr Tung's plan (he liked to be called 'C.Y.' by his devoted employees) was based on an idea first instigated by U. Thant, Secretary General of the United Nations, that a ship be used for educational purposes whilst spreading goodwill and understanding amongst the nations and between different cultures.

C.Y's plan was ambitious: to convert the world's largest ship into the world's largest floating university (which would be on charter to the Chapman College of Orange, California) and carry eighteen hundred students plus eight hundred cruise passengers in great comfort to destinations bordering the Seven Seas. An initial shake-down maiden cruise around the Pacific would be followed by Round the World Cruises to coincide with American Spring and Autumn terms. (A Chinese crew would help alleviate running costs aggravated by the ever increasing price of oil fuel.) Quite wittily, and using a clever pun on his own name, C.Y. decided to name the new ship after himself – *Seawise University*. When not cruising the *Seawise* would be used as a floating campus in the United States.

But first the liner had to be taken from Point A (Port Everglades) to Point B (Hong Kong). It was first reported that the ship could be towed as far as Singapore where there was a dry dock able to accommodate her (the same she had used during the early days of the Second World War) before carrying on under her own steam to the crown colony off mainland China.

However, it was finally decided to steam her all the way and arrangements were made to ready her for the long journey.

A Chinese crew under Captain William Hsuan and Chief Engineer W. C. Cheng were flown to Florida along with workers from C.Y's own shipyard.

As the *Seawise* – the ship that had been the *Queen Elizabeth* – was larger than anything that the Chinese had experienced before, it was felt prudent to invite experienced advisers to assist with readying the ship for her long journey that would take her more than half-way around the world.

Accordingly Commodore Geoffrey Marr and Chief Engineer Ted Philip received invitations to leave their retirements and fly to Florida to rejoin their old ship, which they were delighted to do.

Preparation for departure was already underway by the time they arrived and Geoffrey Marr, arriving on 18th November, a little later than the engineers, was appalled at the mess that he found on board.

The worst job of all was the problem of ridding the ship of 4,000 tons of oil-contaminated water but this was partly achieved after much effort by the Chinese accompanied by much complaint by the local authorities.

Engines were checked and boilers tested but only six out of the twelve boilers were considered functionable for the long voyage.

During two years of near neglect, deterioration had rapidly set in, especially in the fragile boiler tubes, which substantiated the fears of the dozen or so other English engineer advisers that the best way of getting the ship to Hong Kong would still be to tow her there.

Sailing day inevitably changed from the planned-for date in early December to the date estimated by Geoffrey Marr of February 1971 as 600 boiler tubes had to be changed in the six boilers that would be needed to get the *Seawise* to Hong Kong. Engines, too, were repaired; radar, radio and other navigational aids overhauled; testing was undertaken and approval obtained by classification societies on various pieces of equipment; the ship's bottom was cleaned of growth accumulated since December 1968; lifeboats replaced; cables and anchors retrieved from their beddings on shore (where they had acted as additional moorings) and replaced in cable lockers and hawse pipes; and so on and so on and so on.

The first two repaired boilers were flashed-up on New Year's Eve and engine trials were carried out on 3rd February 1971.

At last the day of sailing could be decided. After several days of gales, a lull coinciding with a suitable day-time tide was chosen – Wednesday 10th February.

The day was similar to the one that saw the *Elizabeth* arrive in Port Everglades but with one difference. The *Seawise* was now comparatively underpowered and manned by an inexperienced crew and, should anything amiss occur, the liner would become 'the biggest dam' cork that Port Everglades had ever seen!' as Commodore Marr told the press, much to C. Y. Tung's concern as the statement immediately increased the insurance premiums on the ship!

The *Seawise University* left unmourned from her resting place alongside the undeveloped berths 24 and 25 in Port Everglades. The berths were in the passenger area of the docks and were sited at the southern end of the harbour just inside the busy entrance to the Intracoastal Waterway. The berths had been temporary as it had been planned to move the ship later to a permanent berth further down the waterway. On board the ship as she left the harbour that had welcomed her with so much rapture twenty six long months previously was Port Commissioner W. Phil McConaghey who was making a short trip before disembarking onto one of the accompanying tugs.

The Commissioner, elected to office after the liner's arrival at the Florida port, had been appalled at the slackness of the commercial and leasing agreements that he had inherited from the previous administration.

Quite rightly he reappraised the confused situation and found it to be drastically wanting. Unhappily, especially as he admired the *Elizabeth*, he took his remedying measures to the extreme and, using a helpless 84,000 ton ship as a scapegoat, the symbol of all the ills caused by local mismanagement and political squabbling, became determined to rid the port of her.

Before the *Seawise* even left her berth a message was received by the Bridge that one of the six operational boilers had developed leaks in its tubes during the preceding night and was thus unoperational.

By the time the liner had been taken from the mouth of the Intracoastal Waterway and turned in the harbour of Port Everglades to face towards the 300 foot entrance, another boiler went out of action. Fate, as well as Florida, now seemed to turn her back on the former Queen of the Seas.

Technically the liner did not now have enough power to manoeuvre, should the need arise, but she did have enough momentum – plus the aid of tugs – to carry her through the entrance opening. Advisor Commodore Marr had telephoned his counterpart, Ted Philip, in the Engine Room just before the second boiler blew 'We are committed to the channel now. See that they give her everything they can!' This timely order ensured that the liner just managed to gain enough way to glide through into the open sea without slewing around at the harbour mouth in the 15 knot wind that was blowing.

The fall-off in power also prevented the ship that had been the *Queen Elizabeth* from manoeuvring once out in the open sea. She could not now provide a lee for the tug that came bucking alongside to take off the pilot and her civic passenger.

At least one person on the liner thought that almost poetic justice would be done if the man, who had done so much to rid the port of the hapless liner and send her into a second exile, was pitched into the sea by the giantess from which he was now disembarking!

The next day as the ship proceeded south there was a massive loss of feed water in No. 4 Boiler Room but this was corrected by the British advisers and soon an excess of water was being produced.

But luck again took a downward turn as a serious fire in No. 4 Boiler Room broke out just after 9 am on Saturday 13 February. An hour later the fire had been brought under control but one of the boilers was found to be badly damaged.

Captain Hsuan decided to signal for a tug. Meanwhile the liner drifted helplessly at the mercy of the winds and currents. At night a white light rigged fore and aft and two red lights on the foremast warned other ships that the *Seawise University* was not under control.

The Norwegian cruise liner *Starward* approached the wallowing leviathan just before Sunday midnight, playing on the darkened liner with her brash, bright searchlights. An offer of assistance by the Norwegians was declined by Captain Hsuan as he waited for the tug.

The salvage tug *Rescue* arrived on the following Tuesday as the liner completed her drift down through the Windward Passage between the Scylla and Charybidas of the Caribbean – Fidel Castro's communist Cuba on one side and 'Papa Doc' Duvalier's voodoo-ridden Haiti on the other.

It had been intended to tow the old Cunarder to Jamaica but again wind and tide thwarted the plan. The second choice of Curacao was also abandoned and the small Dutch island, Aruba, was chosen. Situated a few miles off the northern Venezuelan coast, the island had extensive oil-orientated facilities and would make a suitable base for repairs.

But to gain the island a second tug had been summoned and together the two small craft laboriously towed their charge, trailing a quarter of a mile astern, on her Odyssean journey across the Caribbean.

On arrival off Aruba the pilot ordered her to anchor but, after the tugs had left her and before anyone could realise, she had been brought to a halt some way off the planned anchoring ground.

A wind blew up and the *Seawise University* drifted, dragging her anchor, out to deep water.

The trailing anchor bedded itself into an offshore sandbank. Another tug, the *Schelde* out of Oranjestad in Aruba, came out and towed the liner off the relatively safe anchorage of the sandbank and then, under the pretext of having engine trouble herself, cast the *Seawise* adrift and helpless in deeper water hoping, it seemed, to return later to claim salvage.

After enquiries by C.Y. Tung's representatives the *Schelde*, now in harbour, suddenly became free of any problems and, with another tug, *Los Cocos*, towed the *Seawise* to another haven where the liner put down two anchors, six miles from Oranjestad.

Men, boiler tubes and other equipment were flown to Aruba to hasten the liner's repair. C.Y. Tung visited the ship in person and ordered the Boiler and Engine Rooms to be thoroughly cleaned and painted. By the time the two chief advisers returned from a short leave in England they found that the Old Lady was almost her old self.

After seventy-four days spent in a pleasant climate (although with a choppy sea) the British contingent felt that, at long last, the old *Lizzie* was being given a new lease of life. She sailed from Aruba bound for Curacao under her own, now certain, power, lifting her bows to the ocean's swell.

Fresh water and fuel oil were taken on at Curacao and another similar stop was made at Port of Spain on Trinidad.

Speeds varied between a discreet 7 and 11 knots, with the latter speed using 300 tons of bunkers per day.

The British contingent wished that she could be 'opened up' but Captain Hsuan decided to play safe. Also, rather than steam directly for Capetown, he diverted his ship to Rio de Janeiro where she arrived in the early dawn of Sunday 30th May to an interested welcome.

A fortnight later the *Seawise University* arrived to a warm reception in an otherwise windy Capetown which left Geoffrey Marr thinking that the ship would always be welcomed there during her future world cruises.

As the *Seawise* crossed the Indian Ocean, steadily rising and falling to a swell that had other ships dipping their bows in showers of spray, the old Cunard hands were reminded (other than for the speed being made) of the halcyon days on the North Atlantic when the liner was the *Queen Elizabeth*.

A call at Singapore on 7th July brought forth a splendid welcome by aircraft of the RAF but the publicity was kept low-key as her new owners wanted her to be properly welcomed there when she was finally restored, pristine in her new paintwork. (At that time it was anticipated that her hitherto black hull would be painted a light grey, her superstructure would remain white and her funnels painted in Orient Oversea's orange with an applied plum blossom motif.)

The *Seawise University* arrived in Hong Kong after being '... the slowest boat to China' but her performance was such that she arrived early and had to steam around the harbour at slow speed to kill almost a day.

However, on Thursday 15th July the liner was given an early morning welcome by helicopters, a fire boat display and a multitude of small craft bustling around her.

This time the Queen was home and about to embark on a new lease of life.

Gradually, over the next few months C.Y. Tung's great ship was reconditioned and converted into the ship of his dreams. The IMCO fire-fighting standards (that Cunard were not able to afford) were incorporated, bringing the liner into line with the stringent standards that the Americans especially – with all their bitter experiences of years gone by – demanded of foreign vessels.

Two thousand men were shipped out daily to the vessel that was undergoing a gigantic renovation exercise equalling the liner's immediate post-war conversion from troopship to passenger liner on the Clyde in 1946.

By the New Year of 1972 the *Seawise University* floated resplendent in her new livery of white hull and orange funnels, the legend 'Orient Overseas Line' proudly emblazoned along each side of the hull below the Bridge and level with the Main Deck. All twelve boilers had been reconditioned and her four engines thoroughly overhauled. Dry docking in Japan would shortly follow to check, clean and paint her underwater hull and fittings.

Hope sparkled in the clear sunshine of Sunday 9th January. About 540 workmen were left on board, many of the usual 2,000 who were kept busy on the conversion work having already gone ashore for lunch. The ship's catering staff busied themselves preparing for a reception to be hosted that day by C.H. Tung, C.Y's son.

About 11.30 that morning a lone yachtsman, indulging in the pleasures of the harbour and of the day, looked over to the huge, white liner and, to his consternation, saw flames flickering from what appeared to be a pile of rubbish dumped by an open door in the ship's side.

On board, too, other fires were discovered – three at least had started almost simultaneously (there could have been many more) – and these quickly spread, fanned and carried by the ample supply of air coming into the liner through the openings in the hull.

As the ship's fire-fighting crew struggled to control one of the blazes (they were unaware of the existence of the others), the remainder of the crew and the party guests who had already arrived on board hurriedly abandoned ship, some sliding down hawsers to escape the rapidly spreading flames.

Nearing completion as a university cruise ship, the *Seawise University* made a sparkling sight in Hong Kong harbour. The plum-leaf motifs have not yet been attached to her funnels.
John Havers

A whole hour passed after the first cry of 'Fire' before fire-fighting tugs arrived at the scene and started pumping a part of Hong Kong's harbour into the ship, thousands of gallons of water that fell onto the upperworks of the burning ship that had been the *Queen Elizabeth*.

Dense smoke billowed from along the length of the liner as the fire spread, drifting in clouds across to the island city. As the fire took hold, feeding on woodwork, carpets and furniture, and as rare veneers and marquetry blistered, peeled and briefly fed the conflagration within the ship, explosions racked the liner. Her newly-painted hull blistered and flared as the paint pulled away from the influence of the heat within.

After four hours the liner was left to burn herself out, abandoned by those who had wept as they had struggled to save her. By now the weight of water pumped on board

'The Most Mighty of Pyres ...'. Smoke billows across Hong Kong harbour in the early stages of the fire, the liner's hull, as yet relatively unscorched.   *Collection of Robert Lenzer, Richardson, Texas*

by the fire-fighting tugs had caused the liner to list; water started to pour through the open doors near to the water-line.

By midnight of that awful day the fire had burnt through five decks and the liner had developed a list of 17°. Her starboard side was red hot with much of the paintwork completely burnt, exposing the charred steel plates of the dead hull.

Not only had the Chinese inherited the largest liner in the world they had also inherited the spectre of the *Normandie* as the *Seawise University* started a slow and unstoppable capsize.

Twenty-four hours after the discovery of the fires the old *Queen* was resting at an acute angle on the harbour bottom, her upperworks and bridge collapsed inwardly if they had not disintegrated, her funnels blackened, her masts contorted. The fire would burn for another day.

Back in England Geoffrey Marr had by this time learnt with horror that his 'darling' was burning and making headlines worldwide.

At 6.45 on the morning of 10th January the Commodore was annoyed to be awakened by the jingling of the telephone. His annoyance soon disappeared as he answered the instrument.

It was John Timpson of the BBC. Had the Commodore heard that his last Command had just capsized in Hong Kong harbour and did the Commodore want to make any comment?

Almost at a loss Geoffrey Marr recalled Noel Mostert's words which he quoted as an epitaph, ending:

'..... no tanker, no matter what its size, could ever convey the visual impact of these two magnificent ships, especially when seen at speed, flinging aside the North Atlantic in huge combers, their whole line one of power and splendour: oceanic palaces of magnificent proportions'.

John Timpson said simply, quietly:
'Who could follow that?'

The retired Commodore had thought that, as the liner had been four times as large as anything the Chinese had owned before, they were afraid of the ship. At least the Cunard people had become accustomed to leviathans in progressive stages.

He also considered that, as so much money had been expended on the old *Lizzie*'s refit, arson could be the only cause. The Court of Inquiry held later backed up his assessment.

The *Queen* was dead, but the problem now existed that she was an eyesore and a hazard.

A year later she was still there, still rusting. On the first anniversary of the ship's destruction her one time commander, Sir Ivan Thompson, joined a small group of men in a memorial service at the end of Pier 90 in New York. The old *Lizzie* was still missed, still remembered with affection by those who had known her.

She also found fleeting fame as she slept forever. Ian Fleming's famous spy James Bond found British secret headquarters built into the listing liner in the film 'The Man With the Golden Gun'. But that was about as far as romance would touch the old liner as she was laid-out in Hong Kong.

Oil gradually seeped from ruptured fuel tanks and an inflated boom was floated around the rusting hulk to contain it. Two years later 3,000 tons of the stuff would be pumped out at a cost of £140,000 as C.Y. was pressed to move the wreck.

It would have taken millions to salvage and rebuild the liner so in December 1974 the owners decided, sadly and reluctantly, to scrap her.

A month later a memorial to the ship was unveiled by Mayor Lindsay outside Orient Oversea's New York offices in Water Street. Made of granite the memorial contained two eighteen inch letters, 'Q' and 'E', from the liner's name along with carved copies of letters from the Queen Mother and the Secretary General of the United Nations.

The rest of the hull was cut or blown into sections of up to 250 tons each and, in all, 45,000 tons of metal were lifted from the wreck, much of it destined to become reinforcing bars in Hong Kong's changing skyline.

The heat of the fire had also fused glass from porthole lights into their surrounding brass frames and seven hundred pounds of this unusual material was purchased by the Parker Pen Company. As a result a limited, numbered edition of beautiful green/gold, almost sparkling, fountain pens were produced one of which, resplendent in a mahogany casket, was presented to Commodore Marr.

The Korean scrappers, under the guidance of a British engineer, decently buried the remains of the wreck in the sand of the harbour bottom, hoping that they had given the Old Lady a respectful burial.

But even her remains may now not be allowed to rest in peace, as it was hoped, forever.

In a letter to the nautical magazine 'Ships Monthly' (August 1989) Bernard Young of New South Wales, Australia, concluded a letter concerning Hong Kong '... Stonecutters Island, the site of ... wreck of ... *Queen Elizabeth*. Although no longer visible, a large part of the wreck still lies on the sea bed and I understand it is causing some problems for the designers of a proposed new tunnel

Scorched with collapsed steelwork, the *Seawise University* sits dangerously in the water, her lower cargo ports level with the sea.   *Queen Elizabeth Historical Society*

near there. Poor old *Lizzie*, or what is left of her, lies in the way and they have to decide whether to go round her or blow her up.'

'To see thy beauty fade ...
Lovely to the last,
Extinguished, not decayed.'
(Byron)

Almost 35 years from the laying of her keel the old *Queen Elizabeth* reaches an undignified end, a charred, rusting hulk thousands of miles from the land that gave her being.   *Terry Little*

Acknowledgements

The preparation of a ship biography - even a brief one such as this - would not be possible without the help of people directly involved in building, sailing or travelling in the ship concerned. I am indebted, therefore, to those so involved and who so freely gave of their time and of their memories of the *Queen Elizabeth*.

I am particularly grateful to Commodore Geoffrey Marr DSC, RD, RNR (ret'd) for his recollections, for writing the Foreword and for allowing me the honour of dedicating the book to his late wife.

To the Commodore I also extend to a second vote of thanks for reading through the typed manuscript and to Captain Peter Jackson and Kippy Robinson of Hamble for performing a similarly onerous task, although mine is the final responsibility for any errors and omissions.

The anecdotes and recollections that I have collected can only scratch the surface of an apparent wealth of stories, but I hope that I hav e given a flavour of the life on board a great liner through the stories presented. Two other special sources must also not go unacclaimed: firstly Sam Campbell who patiently answered my detailed questions on his own involvement in the building of 'No. 552' and, secondly, Harold Philpot of Ararat, Virginia. Harold is courageously and single - handedly building a museum (RMS Queen Elizabeth Historical Society, Route 1, Box 217 Ararat, Virginia 24053, U.S.A.) dedicated solely to the great ship. To his great enthusiasm and encouragement I owe a great deal.

Many others helped to fill in the gaps with information, photographs and artefacts. I am very mindful of their invaluable contributions and thank them all, including: Peter Ashton; Ian Baker; Stewart Bale Ltd; Len Betts; Peter Boyd-Smith of 'Cobwebs' (Oceanliner Memorabilia) Southampton; George Boyd; Frank O.Braynard of Sea Cliff, New York; the late Len Brown; Simone Clarke; James Collins; Harley Crossley; Cunard Line Limited; William Doig; John Eaton; Jill Fackerell; Eric Flounders; Fotoflite, Ashford, Kent; George Gardner; University of Glasgow Archives; Paul Gosling; Les Gough; Thomas Gough; Bob Bruce Grice; Charles Haas; Charles Harrison of Nairobi; John Havers; Ivan 'Jack' Horner; Imperial War Museum; Norman Jackman; Jim Jone; Tim Jone; Baroness Patricia de Kerbrech; Phyllis Larkin; Sylvia Lee; Robert G. Lenzer of Richardson, Texas; Terry Little ex Cunarder and enthusiast, of 'Oysters' Wine Bar, Southsea; University of Liverpool; Jill MacCullum; the late Mrs Geoffrey Marr; Nicola Massey; Bill Miller of Jersey City, N. J.; William Miller; William H. Mitchell; Captain John Moffatt; Dennis Money; Frieda Moody; Denis Morrell; Nigh's of Ventnor (Mr Denis); George Outram Ltd.; Nigel Overton; Red Funnel Steamers; Philip Rentell; C. P. Richards; Martin Rowland; Gary Smith; Mrs Isobel Sorrell; Southampton City Museums; Southern Evening Echo; Ian Sparshatt; P. E. Spriggs; Lovell H. G. Taylor; Alma Topen; Cedric Wasser: Peter Walters; Captain G. D. Williams; Rodney Wise; and George Wolseley.

At a special luncheon held on board *Queen Elizabeth 2* to commemorate the 50th anniversary of the launch of the "old" *Lizzie*, Her Majesty Queen Elizabeth, the Queen Mother, dined with ex-captains of the three *Queens* as well as those currently in command of *QE2*.
Southern Newspapers plc, Southampton

Bibliography

Should the reader require further details of the career of RMS *Queen Elizabeth* then I can particularly recommend, from the list below, the books by Stevens, Winchester, Potter and Frost, Konings and - of course! - Miller and Hutchings.

The recent 'Destiny's Daughter' by Russell Galbraith is also recommended for its detailed look into the subsequent tale of the *Queen Elizabeth* following her sale - a period that I have only lightly touched upon as she was technically no longer the subject of this book.

Commodore Geoffrey Marr's 'The Queens and I', although rare and out of print, is also eminently readable. Let us hope that it will eventually be re-published.

Bisset, Sir James - Commodore (Angus & Robertson, 1961)

Bonsor, N.R.P. - North Atlantic Seaway (David & Charles, 1975)

Braynard, Frank and Miller, William H. - Fifty Famous Liners (Patrick Stephens Ltd, 1982) Cunard S.S. Co - The Cunarders 1840 - 1969 (Peter Barker Publishing Ltd, 1982)

Galbraith, Russell - Destiny's Daughter (Mainstream Publishing, 1988)

Grattidge, Capt. H. - Captain Of The Queens (Oldbourne, 1956)

Hutchings, David F. - QE2 - A Ship For All Seasons (Kingfisher Railway Productions, 1988)

Hutchings, David F. - Queen Mary - 50 Years Of Splendour (Kingfisher Railway Productions, 1986)

Hyde, Francis E. - Cunard And The North Atlantic 1840 - 1973 (The Macmillan Press Ltd, 1975)

Kludas, Arnold - Great Passenger Ships Of The World, Vol.4: 1936 - 1950 (Patrick Stephens Ltd, 1977)

Lacey, Robert - The Queens Of The North Atlantic (Sidgwick & Jackson, 1973)

Maclean, Commodore Donald - Queens' Company (Hutchinson, 1965)

Mcguire, Joseph B. - The Sea My Surgery (Heinemann, 1957)

Marr, Commodore Geoffrey - The Queens And I (Adlard Coles Limited, 1973)

Miller, William H. - Transatlantic Liners 1945 - 1980 (David & Charles, 1981)

Miller, William H. - Great Cruise Ships And Ocean Liners (Dover Publishing Inc., 1988)

Miller, William H. and Hutchings, David F. - Transatlantic Liners At War - The Story of The Queens (David & Charles, 1985) Rentell, Philip - Historic Cunard Liners (Atlantic Transport Publishers, 1986)

Smallpeice, Sir Basil - Of Comets And Queens (Airlife, 1981)

Southampton City Council - The Queens (Harvey Barton - St. Stephens Publications, 1969)

Stevens, Leonard A. - The Elizabeth, Passage Of A Queen (George Allen & Unwin, 1967)

Thelwell, Commodore Robert G. - I Captained The Big Ships (Arthur Barker, 1961)

Winchester, Clarence - The Queen Elizabeth (Winchester, 1947)

I acknowledge and thank many of the above authors and publishers for some of the quotations used.

Periodicals and newspapers also referred to:

The Daily Telegraph, The Times, Southern Evening Echo, New York Times, The Miami News, The Miami Herald, Fort Lauderdale News, Sun-sentinel, Broward County, Philadelphia Magazine, Ships Monthly, Sea Breezes, Shipbuilding & Shipping Record.

July 1952 and the *United States* passes the Prince's Green at Cowes on her approach to Southampton after taking the Blue Ribband on her maiden voyage. The *Queen Elizabeth*, having left Southampton an hour previously, prepares to pass the US liner in the difficult bend of the Solent channel.

By kind permission of Nigh's